Irish Cases in Entrepreneurship

Volume II

Edited by

COLETTE HENRY
and
PAURIC MCGOWAN

BLACKHALL
Publishing

This book was typeset by ARK Imaging Services for

BLACKHALL PUBLISHING
33 Carysfort Avenue
Blackrock
Co. Dublin
Ireland

e-mail: info@blackhallpublishing.com
www.blackhallpublishing.com

ISBN: 978 1 842181 249

A catalogue record for this book is available from the British Library.

Printed in England by Athenaeum Press Ltd

Foreword

Entrepreneurship and new business creation are the lifeblood of every economy. Not only can such elements help to create new industries, generate employment opportunities and revive disadvantaged areas, but they also develop confidence and promote prosperity. Even with the Celtic Tiger still in our midst, the need for us to continue to create more dynamic Irish entrepreneurs who can start new enterprises and develop existing ones has never been greater.

I never really thought of myself as an entrepreneur, and I probably still don't. Whether you start a new business or develop an existing one you need to be able to be innovative and resilient. I cannot emphasise resilience and positive attitude enough. On the one hand, developing your market, creating opportunities for your product and securing the relevant resources for your business are key entrepreneurial skills that need to be learned and practiced. On the other hand, drive, passion and an ability to work really hard are maybe characteristics that are part of your make-up and not easily acquired. I think it is clear, in this very exciting snapshot of entrepreneurship, that you will do better at what you enjoy. It is very difficult to be passionate about anything unless you believe in what you do. I share the view that while some entrepreneurs are born into this world, others can be encouraged and developed through exposure to learning and role models. While the academic debate about whether entrepreneurs are born or made will no doubt continue, the positive ways in which we can encourage our young people to be innovative and delve into the world of enterprise and entrepreneurship is not be underestimated.

These case studies are live examples of amazing journeys of business stamina, enthusiasm and entrepreneurship. Case studies like these are an interactive and valuable way to learn. The business space comes alive for the reader. The challenges jump off the page, unlike in textbooks. This volume is a very effective way to show and tell the risks and dilemmas of business. The lessons learned form a useful framework for students of Business, Management, Marketing and Entrepreneurship. It is key learning to understand the challenges, issues and problems that entrepreneurs face on a day-to-day basis, as well as the innovative ways these entrepreneurs find to overcome them. Today's generation of Business and Enterprise students need to be exposed to the realities of entrepreneurship. Regardless of the type of business endeavour success is never achieved overnight, and challenges as well as opportunities appear when you least expect them. By studying the successful (and sometimes unsuccessful) strategies of some of our contemporary Irish entrepreneurs, students of any discipline can get a real sense of what it's like to start, manage and develop a business in what is considered to be one of the most supportive entrepreneurial environments in the world.

It is a real privilege to write the foreword to *Irish Cases in Entrepreneurship Volume II*. I admire anyone who is brave enough to tell their business story and allow others to learn off the back of their experiences in business. Case studies, I believe, are like a very enjoyable spectator sport. I hope those of you who want to stay on the sidelines for now will derive real entrepreneurial learning from this volume. Enjoy the read and, maybe, some day soon you will move onto the pitch.

Joanna Gardiner
Managing Director – Ovelle Pharmaceuticals
Chairperson – Dundalk Institute of Technology

INTRE (Ireland's Network of Teachers and Researchers in Entrepreneurship) was initially established in October 2003 when seven people met in Dublin to examine ways in which Irish academics with an interest in entrepreneurship could support each other's activities. Over the two years that followed the network grew to include every third-level institution on the island of Ireland.

INTRE was formally established in January 2006, when its constitution was adopted by the Board, and was officially launched in October 2006 by the Minister for Education, Mary Hanafin. The INTRE Board consists of representatives from each of the 25 third-level colleges who act as champions within their own institution and who disseminate key information arising from the network. A regular e-mail newsletter has been established which offers information about the latest Irish entrepreneurship books, competitions, journals, conferences, calls for research proposals and sources of funding. The principal purpose of the network is to improve the quantity and quality of entrepreneurship research in Ireland and to engender a strong international reputation in this area. Towards achieving this ambition, the following are some of the key objectives that have been identified for the organisation:

- To develop an active network of educators and researchers working in the area of entrepreneurship education.
- To raise the quantity and quality of entrepreneurship education and research.
- To develop and promote high-quality entrepreneurship programmes within the business community locally, regionally and nationally.
- To encourage and promote collaborative work.
- To nurture and encourage the development of academic enterprise.

For further information on INTRE please visit our website: www.intre.ie or e-mail us at: info@intre.ie

Dr Thomas Cooney
Chairman – INTRE

**Centre for
Entrepreneurship
Research**

AT DUNDALK INSTITUTE
OF TECHNOLOGY

Since its establishment in 2001, under the direction of Dr Colette Henry, the Centre for Entrepreneurship Research (CER) has established itself as a national centre for independent, high-level research of relevance to businesses, policy-makers and academics, both nationally and internationally. The CER's small team of researchers comprises both academic and non-academic staff, including external associates from academic institutions in Ireland, mainland Europe and the USA. Collectively, the Centre's research team has published a wide range of articles in the field of entrepreneurship and related areas that have helped inform debate and shape enterprise support interventions.

Based at Dundalk Institute of Technology, the Centre for Entrepreneurship Research continues to add to current knowledge about entrepreneurship generally, whilst setting the agenda for female entrepreneurship research on the island. The Centre disseminates its findings, through publications and research forums, to the wider academic, research and business communities. In addition, the CER provides research opportunities for young researchers and works towards creating an enterprise culture by informing educational programmes.

The Centre for Entrepreneurship Research offers supervision to postgraduate research students working towards Masters and PhD qualifications. In addition, the Centre aims to contribute to the development of Entrepreneurship teaching curricula at undergraduate and postgraduate levels and, recently, through the School of Business Studies it developed a taught Masters programme (MBS) in Entrepreneurship and Marketing.

The Centre for Entrepreneurship Research continuously strives to enhance its understanding of, and contribution to, the field through establishing and maintaining research networks of international excellence. For further information please visit our website: www.entrepreneurshipresearch. com or e-mail us at: info@entrepreneurshipresearch.com

Dr Colette Henry
Director – Centre for Entrepreneurship Research

**NORTHERN IRELAND CENTRE
FOR ENTREPRENEURSHIP**

NICENT was established in 2000 with a commission to promote the entre-preneurship agenda within the higher education sector in Northern Ireland, in particular within the faculties of Science, Engineering and Technology (SET). The initiative, which was initially funded by the Office of Science and Technology (OST) and Invest NI, under the Science Enterprise Challenge, sought to respond to the numerous government strategy documents focusing on the role of the higher education sector in Northern Ireland in promoting the entrepreneurship agenda.

The Centre has sought since its establishment, through the design and delivery of a portfolio of modules and programmes, to build students' awareness of entrepreneurship as a potential career opportunity and to provide support for those individuals and teams who can demonstrate their potential to successfully establish their own new venture. While the intro-duction of entrepreneurship to the curriculum has focused initially on SET faculties NICENT is increasingly widening the appeal to encourage all students within the University of Ulster to view entrepreneurship as a crit-ical part of their career development. All students within the partner insti-tutions are encouraged, for example, to participate in the annual £25,000 Student Enterprise Competition, which is designed to provide them with an opportunity to research the potential of a new business venture. As a consequence of its efforts the NICENT partnership has delivered entre-preneurship education to over 7,000 students within the SET faculties who would not otherwise have received such exposure.

The Centre is currently a partnership between the University of Ulster and Queen's University of Belfast, and retains close working relationships with organisations active in encouraging entrepreneurship in Northern Ireland, such as Invest NI and the Management Leadership Network (MLN). Such networks provide students as well as staff with access to core information and advice on business development issues, funding and support.

For further information please visit our website: www.nicent.ulster.ac.uk
or e-mail us at: nicent@ulster.ac.uk

Dr Pauric McGowan
Director – NICENT

Contents

INTRODUCTION

COLETTE HENRY[1] AND PAURIC MCGOWAN[2]

A core dimension for understanding entrepreneurship is to understand the obsessive opportunity focus of the individual or team of individuals who are the architects of the enterprise they seek to develop. Such individuals are also recognised in extant research to be continuously innovative and comfortable with change. Perhaps the most popular way in which entrepreneurship is understood is in the area of new business venturing. In this context the emphasis is on business start-ups and on identifying and helping individuals to develop the competencies necessary to set up and manage a business enterprise. However, entrepreneurship is also important within more established companies. If such businesses are to remain competitive and continue to grow, given the dynamics of current markets, then they need to find ways of maintaining the entrepreneurial effort of the business. Those managing such businesses need entrepreneurial employees. Indeed, entrepreneurial people are also important in the area of social and community development. Many of Ireland's inner cities and towns are in need of innovative, visionary people who can make a difference to the lives of those around them.

In each of these contexts, that of new business venturing, enterprise development and social entrepreneurship, there is a need for people who have been encouraged to think and behave in entrepreneurial ways and who have the competencies to solve problems and manage change, often in the face of considerable scepticism or even outright opposition. In each context the process of entrepreneurship challenges the individual entrepreneur or members of the entrepreneurial team to obtain and maintain a fit between an opportunity identified in a marketplace, business or community and the resources needed to exploit that opportunity. Entrepreneurial people are persistent, creative, innovative problem-solvers. They are opportunity-focused, calculated risk-takers, people who are comfortable with change and frustrated with the status quo. They are strong communicators, effective negotiators and strong team players. They are people who can combine essential attitudes, such as tolerance of risk and uncertainty, as well a low fear of failure, with key managerial competencies in such a way that helps them to make a difference.

The case studies in this text, the second in a series published by Ireland's Network of Teachers and Researchers in Entrepreneurship (INTRE), provides both the student and teacher of entrepreneurship with an important learning resource for exploring many of the issues introduced above with respect to the entrepreneurial process. Through this collection of case studies the editors have endeavoured to bring together cases from a range of industry sectors, which adopt different approaches to describing business scenarios and highlight a variety of entrepreneurial themes suitable for individual study, in-class discussion or lively debate. The cases in this book are based on businesses of different ages, sizes and structures, led by entrepreneurs from different backgrounds and with contrasting personalities. Collectively, these cases encourage students to consider the strategic choices that entrepreneurs have to face on a daily basis, challenging them to evaluate potential strategies that might move the business forward.

Our first case, EZ Office Supplies, describes the establishment and rapid growth of an office supplies and design company. The perspectives of three different people who interact with the business are presented. Each plays a different role in the business and takes a different view of the way the business is progressing. Subsequently, each of the three people – the founding entrepreneur, the company's financial controller and the local bank manager – has his/her own particular concerns about the business and its future direction. This is an extremely challenging case in which the author, Garvan Whelan, presents a complex set of business and strategy issues. The case is based on the activities of an actual company, but the names of the individuals and the type of business have been changed in order to preserve the confidentiality of the persons involved. Finance, marketing and managing growth are the key discussion points in the case.

Our second case, Doagh Isle Visitor Centre by Sharon Porter, relates the story of a popular visitor attraction in County Donegal. Located on the Inishowen Peninsula, Doagh Isle is undoubtedly situated in one of the most isolated and disadvantaged regions of the country. The case focuses on the entrepreneur and the incredible challenges he had to overcome to turn his ambitious idea into reality. Similar to the first case, marketing and funding are key issues in the case; however the operating environment of the entrepreneur would appear to be more challenging. The notion of overcoming difficulties, self-belief and sheer hard work are the key discussion points in this case.

The Morgan Institute is the subject of our third case, and our first female entrepreneur in the collection. Brenda Morgan, founder of this educational business, was an experienced teacher before embarking on her entrepreneurial journey. The case describes how she started the business in the summer of 2003 and, through an intensive enterprise support programme, developed a business plan that would help this mother of four young children bring her idea to fruition. The growth of the business and the challenges Brenda has met along the way are described. The case authors, Breda O'Dwyer and Ann Sears, highlight the role of the entrepreneur and the future strategic direction of the business as key issues for discussion.

By way of contrast, our fourth case presents a pre-start-up scenario. The case author, Tom Cooney, relates the story of three students at Dublin Institute of Technology who, as part of their course work, were asked to identify a business opportunity and prepare a business plan. The result was the proposed 'Guardian Angel' product, a combined natural gas, CO (carbon monoxide) and smoke detection system. Interestingly, this case is presented in the form of a detailed business plan, which evaluates the business opportunity and describes exactly how the business will operate under the management of the three young aspiring female entrepreneurs. The case discusses all the major issues that an entrepreneur has to consider before starting a business and is a good example of the level of research that needs to be undertaken in order to prepare a robust business plan for consideration by venture capitalists. The issue of investment is paramount here, as, without the necessary funds, the business will not move forward.

Our fifth case, the first of three cases within the food sector, is based on O'Briens Sandwich Bars. Founded in the 1980s, O'Briens has developed from a small start-up business into an international brand, mainly through franchising. The case authors, Chris O'Riordan, James Cunningham and Denis Harrington, describe the early years of the O'Briens enterprise, discussing the product, the market and the competition. The company's successes as well as its failures are related. The corporate and social responsibility (CSR) aspect adds an interesting dimension to the case, with CSR strategies operating at store and corporate level. In addition, marketing, customer focus, internationalisation and franchising are the key themes discussed in this robust case.

The Butler's Pantry, our sixth case, is again based on the food sector. Established in 1987 by Eileen Bergin, the company has developed a reputation as a high-quality producer and retailer of 'food to go'. The business has grown rapidly from sales of just twelve meals on its first day of retailing, to nearly 2,000 meals daily and a variety of breads and desserts. Geraldine Lavin, the case author, describes the market for the business and illustrates how the brand was built through steady growth over nearly twenty years. The sorts of skills needed for success in business are discussed, and the importance of a focused business strategy is highlighted as a key theme within the case. Maintaining the integrity of the Butler's Pantry brand while building new business becomes the key challenge for the company.

We stay with the food industry for our final case, Glenisk, which is authored by Geraldine McGing and Pauline Connolly. Developed from a family-run business, Glenisk produces a wide range of organic dairy products utilising fully certified Irish organic milk. The case describes the background to the establishment and growth of Glenisk in the lead up to its new partnership deal with Stonyfield Europe. The case authors outline Glenisk's product range and discuss its market and key competitors. Marketing strategy is a key focus of the case and the reader is left wondering whether the company's new strategic partner will eventually make a bid to buy out Glenisk entirely. Growth and the investment required to fund growth plans are also key discussion points presented by the case.

We expect that this text will become a valuable resource for both teachers and students of entrepreneurship. As a follow-on to INTRE's highly successful book of case studies published in 2005,[3] this second volume of *Irish Cases in Entrepreneurship* helps to identify the pathways and strategies of aspiring and established Irish entrepreneurs, thus providing real insights into the new venture creation and management process.

Colette Henry
Pauric McGowan

NOTES

[1] Dr Colette Henry is Head of the Department of Business Studies and Director of the Centre for Entrepreneurship Research (CER) at Dundalk Institute of Technology.

[2] Dr Pauric McGowan is Director of the Northern Ireland Centre for Entrepreneurship (NICENT) at the University of Ulster at Jordanstown.

[3] Cooney, Thomas M. (ed.) (2005) *Irish Cases in Entrepreneurship*, Dublin: Blackhall Publishing, ISBN: 978 184218 0877.

EZ Office Supplies & Design Services[1]

GARVAN WHELAN[2]

Long after everyone else had left the office, Eamonn Kelly sat behind his mahogany desk and read, with quiet satisfaction, a newspaper headline that proclaimed him as a "Local Hero". The article went on to describe how Eamonn had started EZ Office Supplies and Design Services Limited (EZ) just over three years ago, and with "hard work and perseverance" he had now built up a successful business with sixteen employees and an annual turnover in excess of €5 million.

Eamonn was planning further expansion, but he knew that the company needed to "sort out its finances". He was working late because he had to review a draft business plan that had been prepared by Anne, the company's financial controller. This document had been requested by Brendan, his local bank manager, and would be discussed at a meeting the next day.

Early the next morning Anne O'Driscoll arrived at her office in order to prepare for that meeting. She had worked hard to complete the draft business plan. Anne knew that Eamonn hadn't read most of it, but she was determined to know every detail it contained so that she would be ready for any queries Brendan might have.

Later that morning Brendan Murphy was also preparing for the meeting. He was pleased that the company had grown so rapidly. EZ was now one of his largest clients, and 'add-on' business in the form of leasing and debt factoring helped to increase branch profits. However, he was concerned that the company's overdraft was often in excess of its agreed limit, and he had informed Eamonn that the company needed to restructure its finances. Brendan had suggested that they hold a meeting so that they could make progress on a number of issues with a view to finalising the business plan.

Each of the three people attending the meeting viewed the purpose of preparing a business plan from a different perspective:

- Eamonn – "to keep the banks happy" and as an opportunity to articulate his views on the company's future strategic direction.
- Anne – to clarify which areas of the business required funding.
- Brendan – to help him decide on whether to recommend granting a €200,000 loan as requested by the company.

In order to complete a report for his regional lending manager, Brendan needed to review the company's financial performance and position over the last three years and to briefly outline the background of the key players and their association with the company. As they sat around the table of Eamonn's new boardroom each of them recalled how they became involved with the company, and contemplated the milestones in the remarkable progress of the firm's growth – as recorded in the notes taken by Anne from previous annual reviews.

BACKGROUND

Eamonn

Eamonn is the eldest of seven children and the son of a self-employed shopkeeper and newsagent. His mother "looked after the family, worked in the shop and also did most of the paperwork". His early childhood was fairly happy but, as he grew older, he had frequent arguments with his father. At school he was an average student and would have been considered "a bit of a loner". He was not very interested in doing well at exams, but managed to obtain his Leaving Certificate. His parents hoped he would complete a degree in Commerce, but he did not have enough points. Instead, he enrolled for an Arts degree, with a major in Economics. He failed his exams at the end of second year, had a major row with his father, left home and went to London, where he stayed initially with relatives.

His uncle owned a successful construction company there and gave him work as a labourer on the condition that he found another job within six months. He was advised to attend night classes by the same person, who thought that Eamonn was not suited to a lifetime on the building sites. Eamonn had always enjoyed art at school and so decided to enrol on a course in Graphic Design. Thereafter, he supported himself by working in bars and restaurants and, after two years, he obtained a certificate in Design and started to work for an advertising agency. He was very successful in this career, and supplemented his income by undertaking consultancy work for clients introduced to him by his uncle. He also found that he had a flair for sales, and often received large bonuses for securing new customers and selling extra services to existing clients.

He became friendly with a sales representative who sold computer and office supplies to the firm that Eamonn worked for in London and, after seven years, he returned home with £50,000 sterling to his name and an idea for making big money in Ireland. He had learned that there was a huge difference between the wholesale and retail prices for these goods. Eamonn secured the agency for Ireland for a line of computer and office supplies from a wholesaler based in London. His idea was to sell these products on a retail *and* wholesale basis, and to supplement his income by undertaking graphic design work for those clients who had ordered office supplies.

Exhibit 1.1
The Office Supplies Market

The office supplies and services market consists of revenues generated from the manufacture and sale of paper, storage equipment, pens and pencils, business forms and stationery, and office services, such as photocopying, printing, binding, etc.

 In line with a strong, booming economy, the Irish office supplies and services market has experienced strong growth over the 1999–2004 period, with a compound annual growth rate (CAGR) of 9.8 per cent. Looking ahead, the market is predicted to experience steady growth of 6.4 per cent over the next few years, which is at a stronger pace than the predicted UK and European market CAGR of 2.4 per cent. The expanding Irish market is likely to attract competition from overseas and online suppliers with resulting pressure on selling prices and profit margins.

Companies that specialise in office supplies business are also facing increased competition from retailers such as general merchandisers, grocery chains, discount stores, etc., who are increasingly stocking office products in their stores. However, these 'specialist' firms are able to fight back by offering a wider range of products and by increasing their economies of scale through the use of bulk discounts and sourcing products from low cost producers in developing economies.

Sources: Datamonitor, 2005 Report on the Office Services and Supplies Market, and interviews with key industry informants.

Exhibit 1.2
The Role of Graphic Design

As business has been transformed over the last decade by the advent of digital media, graphic design has taken on a powerful new role. Traditionally, in the power hierarchy of industry, manufacturers held sway. The means of production, the factory, was the power base which the other parts of the business cycle, such as the customer or design and marketing, were subsidiary to. In the era before marketing assumed its appropriate place at the centre of the business, companies produced first and then sought markets through distributors.

Later, as marketing became inculcated into the business culture, a more significant role was given to the designer, since the marketing people were advising the producer exactly what the market/customer wanted. Designers were now being employed but their contribution was not seen as significant, and respect for what was seen as an expense was given grudgingly. Graphic designers had, throughout this period, always been regarded as useful for producing colourful brochures or leaflets, but their presence was tolerated usually as an expensive, cosmetic afterthought.

With the advent of the Internet and online business, and the ubiquitous availability of a wide variety of most products, the tide has turned for most manufacturers. They no longer hold predominance. The availability of products in consumer markets is more or less a given. On the Internet the choice is so wide that consumers can find several alternatives to suit their needs, price range and any permutation of features that may be required.

The designer has now taken centre stage. Now we are talking not about the random possibility of including design in the business plan, but the impossibility of not doing so.

Source: http://www.designireland.ie/resources.asp?id=184

Anne

Anne is the second eldest of four children. Her father was an accountant. Her mother was a legal secretary but became a full-time homemaker after the birth of her third child. Anne had a "fairly normal" childhood and got on reasonably well with both her parents. She did very well in her Leaving Certificate exams and went to a nearby Institute of Technology where she received a degree in Business Studies. After that Anne secured a job as a trainee with a large firm of accountants. She qualified after three years but was dissatisfied with her prospects for promotion and so moved to a smaller firm in her home town. It was while working with this firm that she first came across Eamonn's business. As the Audit Senior, Anne was sent out to EZ to help prepare for an inspection by the Revenue Commissioners regarding the company's VAT and PAYE returns. There, Eamonn asked her to help him out by getting the accounts and his tax affairs up to date. At the time, he could not afford a full-time accountant.

Brendan

Brendan is the younger of two children. Both parents worked in the banking sector. Apart from the upset caused by moving home twice in his teenage years, Brendan had a happy childhood. He got on well with both of his parents, especially his father, with whom he shared an interest in sport. He did an Arts degree in college, where he first met Eamonn. Shortly after graduating he followed his parents' footsteps and entered the banking world. He spent three years at headquarters in Dublin and there completed his Institute of Bankers' Exams. He was then transferred to different locations throughout the country and had just been promoted to branch manager when he met Eamonn, who had recently returned from England.

YEAR ONE: START-UP

Eamonn

Eamonn found the start-up phase "very exciting" but more difficult than he had envisaged. There were numerous snags and obstacles that had to be overcome before he could concentrate on his main strengths – sales and design. For instance, there were several issues that had arisen in finalising the contract with his main UK supplier. Prior to this he had never heard of letters of credit, but now he had to organise and finance one every month. He was also surprised at how insistent the UK supplier was on minimum quantities that had to be ordered each quarter in order to secure bulk discounts. However, in spite of these difficulties, he felt that the company had performed reasonably well, as evidenced by the volume of sales, which were in excess of his initial targets. Eamonn was especially pleased that he had obtained repeat orders from several of the larger companies in the town. Some of them had even provided testimonial letters, stating that they were impressed with the competitive prices and the broad range of products available from EZ. Eamonn therefore thought that, having dealt with all of the "technical hitches" in the first year, the company was in a good position to expand by opening up two more retail outlets in other locations.

Anne

Anne started working for EZ Office Supplies and Design Limited on a part-time basis four months after the company commenced trading. Eamonn was so busy that, before the end of the year, he offered Anne a position as office manager. This meant that she was responsible for the company's administration, including cash sales, debtors, creditors and wages. In her opinion, the company had performed reasonably well in its first year of trading, showing a small profit. Its financial position was also satisfactory, as the balance sheet showed a healthy surplus of assets over liabilities.

Brendan

Brendan was glad that he met Eamonn when he did. Having been just promoted to branch manager, it was important to secure the business of new, fast-growing companies like EZ. In addition, he was often asked along to various meetings and social events organised by Eamonn. This enabled him to meet the company's new customers, some of whom transferred their business to Brendan's bank. As far as he was concerned, the company had performed well over the first year, with turnover on the account exceeding expectations. He was unclear about the basis used to calculate the values of the various assets, but was generally satisfied with the financial position, since any liabilities outstanding were secured on the company's premises.

YEAR TWO: HIGH GROWTH AND PROFITABILITY

Eamonn

Eamonn was visibly excited as he reviewed his financial performance. In all modesty, he claimed that the company's achievements were extraordinary, as sales and staff levels had trebled over the previous year. Profits had also increased. He admitted that costs needed to be controlled but he felt that measures recently introduced by Anne would soon help improve matters. He also divulged that some of his success was attributable to "luck and a little bit of trickery".

Through a chance encounter with an old friend he learned of a company operating a similar business that was in difficulty and, therefore, open to offers to be bought as a going concern. By using contacts in Ireland and the UK, he was able to get accurate figures on the company's profits and levels of debt. Using this information judiciously, he was able to negotiate a rock-bottom price for the company's stocks, customer list and long-term lease agreements on two premises situated in prime locations in busy towns. He set up another retail store and appointed two agents for the company's range of products in areas where he thought it would not be worthwhile to establish retail outlets. The end result of all of this was that EZ was now able to avail of maximum levels of bulk discounts from the UK supplier. This put the company in an excellent position to take on the larger players in the market, since it now had a further advantage over its competitors in the areas of price and product range.

Exhibit 1.3
Competitors – Office Supplies

Viking Direct

Viking Direct is a global company, established in 1960 and now present in over sixteen countries worldwide.

Viking has sold a wide range of office supplies to Irish customers since 1994, and also has offices spread throughout the UK. Its Irish headquarters are in Dublin, with additional premises across the UK in London, Manchester, Glasgow, Edinburgh and several other cities.

The company's catalogue is widely distributed to organisations and businesses and customers can order goods in four different ways:

- Free Phone
- Mailbox
- Free Fax
- Internet

With over 15,000 office products available, Viking can accommodate a wide range of client stationery needs …from pens, paper, office machines and ink cartridges through to warehouse and janitorial supplies.

Source: http://www.vikingdirect.ie/

Bryan S. Ryan

Incorporated in 1948, Bryan S. Ryan is an Irish-owned company employing over eighty people from its headquarters in Dublin. The company supplies office equipment, furniture and stationery to companies throughout Ireland. Bryan S. Ryan has over fifty years experience in assisting customers to reduce their office equipment and stationery costs. The focus is on helping customers to reduce the costs associated with such items as printing, copying, stationery and communications.

Its computerised ordering and stock control system allows their staff to quickly and accurately process and monitor orders. Like

Viking Direct, they provide free (subject to terms and conditions) next day delivery on all stationery orders.

The company's stationery catalogue contains over 15,000 items for the office and they also stock a wide range of printing supplies and computer consumables.

Source: http://www.bryansryan.ie/

Exhibit 1.4
Competitors – Graphic Design

Martec

Established in 1996, Martec provides a wide range of graphic design, website development and Internet marketing services. From its base in Galway the company has worked with companies and organisations from a vast range of industries and backgrounds, including the following categories:

- Business Consulting and Financial Services
- Construction and Property
- Government and Educational Organisations
- High Tech
- Hotels and Restaurants
- Manufacturing
- Non-Profit Organisations
- Retail
- Service Industry

Martec's graphic design service is suitable for individuals and organisations at either a start-up or business development stage. The service related to printed materials and marketing incorporates logo design, photography and graphic illustration for stationery and advertising material.

Their web design service can be tailored for affordable entry-level homepages or flexible, easy to manage, updateable websites. Martec has expertise in content management and developing complex web-based applications, including Flash animation multimedia and E-business marketing solutions.

Source: http://www.martec.ie/

Artefact

This company is a recently established design-led marketing communications agency. Artefact is based in Clontarf, Dublin.

They do not employ sales/account executives. Artefact encourages its clients to deal directly with their designers. In this way, clients do not have to suffer the 'Chinese whispers' effect whereby the brief provided works its way from account executives, through art directors to graphic designers and copywriters and back again.

Artefact prides itself on hiring the best designers who are stakeholders in the business. Their objective is to provide top quality designs for corporate literature, annual reports, websites and packaging. This is done by developing excellent creative concepts, writing smart persuasive copy, and executing the design and artwork to a standard that matches or exceeds the best available in the market.

The company's clientele includes several substantial, blue-chip corporations.

Source: http://www.artefact.ie/

Anne

Anne found the second year of trading to be extremely challenging. Increased turnover and staffing levels meant that there was now a considerable amount of administrative work to be completed every day. A bookkeeper and office assistant had been hired, but Anne felt that she hardly had the time to train them properly.

With Eamonn's guidance, Anne had recently introduced a bonus scheme for all sales staff, which had helped to increase turnover. She pointed out that the gross profit margin of 50 per cent indicated an improved trading performance. She had also rationalised the sales territories to cut down on unnecessary travel. This, combined with stricter controls on all expense claims, was expected to help improve operating performance.

Anne felt that it was more difficult to assess the company's true financial position because, at that stage – three months after the second year of trading had expired – the company's balance sheet had still not been finalised. However, she was confident that total assets were significantly larger than total liabilities, and that the company's financial situation was secure. Anne also commented that she had expressed concern to Eamonn regarding the high levels of stock and debtors. He had replied that a certain amount of this was to be expected as the company sought to improve its market share. He asked Anne to investigate this further and to report back with proposed solutions.

Brendan

Brendan had mixed views regarding the company's financial performance and position. He was pleased with the increased business and the new accounts opened in the company's name over the previous year, but was worried that the company seemed incapable of operating within agreed overdraft limits. The name of EZ Office Supplies and Design Limited was starting to appear on his *Out of Order Report* (which highlighted 'troublesome' accounts) on a regular basis. His *Hardcore Report* (which calculated the difference between lodgements and payments in the current account) showed a large net cash-flow deficit. He felt that this was jeopardising the company's credibility with the bank. He had asked Eamonn to meet him to discuss the situation but the latter had postponed the meeting twice, citing the pressures of dealing with new and existing customers as the reason for the delays. Brendan's regional manager was already of the opinion that the company had grown too fast and that Eamonn was "in danger of over-extending himself". When this was mentioned to the latter, he retorted quickly that "bank managers don't understand the real business world" and that "opportunities had to be seized, otherwise they would be lost". Brendan was getting worried.

YEAR THREE: GETTING ESTABLISHED IN THE MARKET

Eamonn

Eamonn was very proud of the company's financial performance in its third year of trading. He felt that they had improved and consolidated their position, as sales and profits had once again increased. This growth was attained through further expansion of the branch network – another retail store was opened – and the appointment of two new agents. This enabled Eamonn to increase the quantities ordered from suppliers and, thus, negotiate higher levels of bulk discounts and more generous credit terms. The design consultancy was also very successful and helped to attract new customers for office and computer supplies. Recently, he had "pulled off a major publicity coup" by officially opening the new retail outlet in conjunction with his company receiving an award for Distributor of the Year from his main UK supplier. He boasted of how "there was no such award" and that the UK supplier went along with his idea because "it figured the publicity would boost sales". The publicity surrounding the event emphasised two main themes:

1. Eamonn's contribution to the region as a provider of employment (he had twenty-four employees at the time).
2. The company's wide range of products and services were priced lower than his main competitor – a larger organisation that was longer established.

In Eamonn's opinion, the company's reputation and its capacity to change by offering new products and services were its greatest resources. He also pointed out that the increasing value of the premises owned by the company was further evidence of the firm's strong financial position.

Anne

As part of the public relations campaign in the local press and radio, Anne also received publicity for her use of technology as part of an improved stock order and control system. This had significantly reduced the stock turnover period by one third (from 65 to 42 days). She had also uncovered some minor leakage of high-value stock items. Other positive improvements in financial performance included an increased gross profit margin (52 per cent) and a reduced overtime-to-wages ratio (down to 38 per cent in Year Three, from 49 per cent in the previous period).

Anne was, by then, the Financial Controller and had co-signing authority on the company's current bank account. Like Brendan, she was becoming concerned about the company's increasing bank overdraft. Also, the amounts of both debtors and creditors had significantly increased, and some of the Irish suppliers had threatened legal action. Eamonn had laughed at "their neck" and commented that "some of them had come practically begging for his business". He pointed out that there were queries outstanding on some of the invoices, which could account for the delay in payment. Eamonn was still responsible for dealing with creditors and promised to clear up any misunderstanding. As regards the overall financial position, Anne reiterated that the balance sheet still showed a healthy net asset position.

Exhibit 1.5
Extracts from Financial Statements and Key Ratios

Table 1.1: **Extracts from Financial Statements**

	2003 €000s	2004 €000s	2005 €000s
Sales – Office Supplies	796	2,471	4,561
Sales – Graphic Design	33	197	623
Sales – Total	829	2,668	5,184
Director's Salary	80	125	200
Current Assets	208	753	1,758
Current Liabilities	147	632	1,334
Net Current Assets	61	121	424

Table 1.2: **Key Ratios**

	2003	2004	2005
	%	%	%
Gearing (Debt/Total Capital)	25	37	54
Gross Profit as % of Sales	48	50	52
Overtime as % of Wages	36	49	38
	Days	**Days**	**Days**
Credit Allowed to Customers	63	84	87
Credit Received from Suppliers	37	56	74
Stock Turnover Period	45	65	42

Brendan

The Irish suppliers were not the only creditors who were losing patience with Eamonn. At times, Brendan found Eamonn very exasperating to deal with. The previous year had seen a huge increase in turnover on the company account, but cheques and debits had exceeded lodgements. To make matters worse, Eamonn was not keeping him informed of when he needed extra credit. This was putting pressure on Brendan because many of the bank's operations were now centralised, and any decision to increase an overdraft limit now had to be sanctioned at the regional office. This required a report from Brendan, which took time to prepare, and there was usually a delay in getting a decision back from the regional manager. This all meant that the local branch needed to know at least a month in advance if there was a need for extra credit. Many of the outgoings from the company's account were fixed (wages, rent, lease payments, etc.), but the amounts payable to the UK supplier varied significantly from month to month. In Brendan's view, the company's financial position was difficult to evaluate because of the huge fluctuations (mainly in the wrong direction) of the company's bank account. He had met with Eamonn on several occasions in the previous year, when his concerns were duly noted and it was agreed to convert some of the overdraft into a term loan. Eamonn also disclosed that there was a third party who was interested in becoming involved in the company, which would mean a large investment of funds into the business. In the meantime, the company held a clearance sale, which brought in a large amount of cash and brought the account back within its authorised limit.

FUTURE DIRECTION: CONCLUSION OF THE MEETING

After reviewing the financial performance of the company, the parties now had to decide on its future strategy. Eamonn wanted to exploit opportunities in the areas of web-based design services and export markets. He had recently completed a course in Design Technology and believed that the Internet offered access to new, profitable markets. Furthermore, the company's principal wholesaler for office supplies in the UK was ready to appoint a main distributor for Eastern Europe. Eamonn felt that, with his experience of establishing retail outlets and appointing agents, he could take on this task.

Anne proposed that priority be given to ongoing working capital requirements and the introduction of a new computerised control system. This was a type of an Enterprise Resource Planning (ERP) system and would enable the integration of all functions of the business. It would mean that she could track and control each order and item of expenditure. As it was, suppliers were complaining about late payments and customers were annoyed because their orders were not being delivered on time.

In spite of his reservations concerning the company's overdraft, Brendan was keen to finance the company's future plans, not least because the bank held security on its assets. He knew that Eamonn and Anne had done their homework and were aware that other financial institutions were interested in doing business with them at very competitive rates. When asked for his opinion on the likelihood of approval for the €200,000 loan, Brendan said that there was a possibility that the regional office would approve half of that amount with the balance up for consideration after six months. Since each of the four proposed projects would cost approximately €50,000 each, this meant that the company would need to rank them in order of strategic importance.

As they were discussing which projects should be prioritised, Eamonn's mobile phone rang. He explained that he needed to take the call because it was a potential customer who might be placing a large order for design services. Eamonn placed the phone on loudspeaker. When the caller enquired how the business was going, Eamonn replied, "It's great – my accountant was just telling me that we can't keep up with orders!" After a few minutes, the call finished and Eamonn said that they would have to continue the meeting at a later date, but that he would not be available for another week – he was going to London early the next morning and was then flying on to Vilnius in Lithuania.

It was agreed to meet again in two weeks' time in order to finalise the business plan and to decide on future strategy and direction. After the others had left the boardroom, Anne reviewed her notes and summarised the main discussion points for the next meeting.

- Future strategy – Continued growth or consolidation?
- Project priority – How should these four projects be ranked?
  - Web-based design service
  - Overseas expansion of office supplies business
  - Working capital requirements
  - Computerised control system
- Financing – Will Brendan's bank approve the €200,000 loan? What should they do if only €100,000 was forthcoming immediately?

NOTES

1. This case was written as a basis for class discussion rather than to illustrate either effective or ineffective handling of an administrative situation. The case is based on the activities of an actual company. However, in order to preserve the confidentiality of those involved, names and some details have been altered.

2. Garvan Whelan lectures at the Institute of Technology Tallaght (ITT) Dublin.

DOAGH ISLE VISITOR CENTRE[1]

SHARON PORTER[2]

As one approaches the Doagh Isle Visitor Centre one is instantly impressed by two sights – the size of the car park and the view. Looking across the ample car parking area towards the magnificent Five Finger Strand, I wonder what level of entrepreneurial ingenuity it must have taken to turn this venture, located in such a remote corner of Donegal, into one of the most popular visitor attractions in the county (*Inish Times*, 2005).

With this thought in mind, I am welcomed to the Centre by Mr Pat Doherty, the entrepreneur behind the venture. When asked if he is busy, Pat points out six buildings that he is about to start thatching. He has just finished painting them in preparation for the new season, which opens in a couple of weeks' time. While the work Pat has put into the start-up phase of the Doagh Isle Centre is undoubtedly a credit to his entrepreneurial flair and determination, there are clearly a number of challenges that lie ahead. Somehow, I have a feeling that I am keeping the man back from a very busy day, but in the unhurried manner that is so characteristic of this part of Ireland, I'm invited in for a cup of tea and a chat.

INTRODUCTION

The Doagh Isle Visitor Centre is located on the Inishowen Peninsula, County Donegal, close to the most northern point of the Republic of Ireland, Malin Head. County Donegal spans a total area of 1,193,621 acres. It is bounded to the north and west by the Atlantic Ocean, and to the east and south-east by the counties of Derry, Tyrone, Fermanagh and Leitrim. It is the only county in Ireland to have a border of 140km with

17

Northern Ireland, and only 9km with the Republic. The Donegal coastline is the longest in the country at 1,134km.

The county is largely rural in character, interspersed with small and medium-sized towns such as Letterkenny, Buncrana, Ballyshannon, Donegal town and Carndonagh. The majority of these act as localised service centres, with the commercial and administrative activity for Donegal tending to concentrate in Lifford or Letterkenny.

As the most northerly county, Donegal is far removed from the country's capital, and consequently is disadvantaged in many respects. Acute peripherality and isolation have been induced by the county's location, physical distance from major urban centres and the absence of accessible natural hinterlands due to confinement within natural and political boundaries. Geographical isolation has been exacerbated by a poor road infrastructure and low levels of state transport services in the region. Debilitating social and economic consequences have also been wrought by the political border with Northern Ireland.

Indeed, the presence of the Border has acted to sunder the region of Inishowen, in particular, from its natural social and economic hinterland of Derry. Exceptionally high levels of social and economic deprivation and acute peripherality, from both the rest of Ireland and Europe, have combined to characterise this peninsula as one of the most disadvantaged areas of the country. So much so that it has been described as:

> The most disadvantaged of all rural partnership areas supported through the Operational Programme for Local Urban and Rural Development (Inishowen Partnership Co., 2000).

Inishowen is renowned for its barren, rugged coastline and wild scenery. Making a living in this part of Ireland has never been easy. In recent years a decline in the traditional industries such as farming, fishing and textile manufacturing has contributed to high levels of out-migration and unemployment far beyond the national average.

BACKGROUND

The Doagh Isle Visitor Centre is located on farmland, which was traditionally worked by the Doherty family. Pat Doherty, the entrepreneur behind the development of the Centre, lived in one of the cottages on the farm until the mid-1990s. Pat, himself, raised suckling cows on the land. However, farming was not generating a sufficient income to be sustainable. Before this, Pat's father bred rabbits on the land for export to the UK market. Unfortunately, the disease myxomatosis put an end to this line of business for the family.

Pat, like so many of his peers, left school at the age of thirteen. He started working in the construction industry as a labourer and plasterer. He has worked throughout the North and South of Ireland as well as in Germany. In 1993 Pat started working in Dublin with a security company which supplied gates. This job saw him travel the length and breadth of Ireland installing and fixing electronic gates. What he saw while travelling around the south-west of Ireland in particular developed his interest in tourism. He witnessed the large numbers of tourists visiting counties such as Cork, Kerry and Galway and began to question why the north-west was receiving so few tourists in comparison. His travels also made him realise how good the scenery and natural resources of the north-west are in comparison to the rest of the country.

Having worked away from home for many years and having escaped a number of 'near-accidents' on our roads, Pat decided that he needed to do something else with his life that would enable him to live full-time in Inishowen. With a growing awareness of the value of tourism and an interest in his local heritage, Pat spotted an opportunity that would enable him, hopefully, to do just that.

He began to restore the home cottage on the family farm as a visitor attraction in 1997. He also renovated an old barn for use as a teahouse. 1997 was also the 150th anniversary of the Great Famine, which happened in Ireland between 1846 and 1851. During this dark period of Irish history, about a million people are estimated to have died of starvation and epidemic disease. In little more than a decade (1845–55) some two million people emigrated from our shores.

The commemorative events that were held in 1997 and the media attention that they received helped plant the seed in Pat's mind for a visitor centre that would focus on the Irish Famine. Pat was keen not only to develop a sustainable tourist attraction in the area but one that would also focus the public's attention on the fact that famine is still rife today in many parts of the world. This is a strong feature of the centre, evident on the website and on the interpretative signage you see as you tour the Village. Poignant reminders that we can each have a positive impact on the relief of global famine! This message also highlights the organisation's values and the fact that Pat wishes to develop a venture that not only has profit-making objectives but also has a strong social orientation.

INDUSTRY OVERVIEW

According to Fáilte Ireland:

> Tourism is one of the largest and most important components of indigenous industry within the Irish economy. Not alone is tourism a major contributor in generating foreign earnings and sustaining employment, it also plays an important role in developing rural economies and contributing to spatial balance (Fáilte Ireland, 2005, p. 5).

The last decade has seen the tourism industry develop in maturity and importance in the Irish economy, while still characterised by the dominance of individual, small to medium-sized enterprises competing in an increasingly globalised international tourism marketplace. Indeed, the Tourism Policy Review Group of the Department of Arts, Sport and Tourism stated recently that Irish tourism is, arguably, "the most important sector of Irish-owned enterprise since the foundation of the State". The statistics highlight this. The tourism industry in Ireland employs almost 150,000 workers. 6.7 million overseas visitors spent €4.3 billion here in 2005. This level of foreign revenue earnings equals half the value level of exports by all Irish-owned manufacturing companies (Tourism Action Plan Implementation Group, 2006).

However, the picture in Donegal is quite different. In spite of its breath-taking scenery, abundant heritage and high-quality beaches, the county's tourism sector continues to be one of the weakest contributors to the real per capita income of the region. Poor physical infrastructure and access, inadequate marketing, and lack of accommodation and entertainment services are among the reasons cited for this continuing trend. While these factors are admittedly significant barriers to the development of the industry, the impact of the political border plays a dominant role in impairing Donegal's position in the tourism market.

A report on the regional spread of tourism, published by the Irish Tourism Industry Confederation in 2005, highlights such significant variations in regional tourism performance in recent years. Between 1999 and 2004 the number of additional bed-nights spent by overseas holidaymakers in Dublin increased by more than 3 million to nearly 7.5 million. However, elsewhere in the country the number of visitor bed-nights actually fell by 2.5 million (to almost 16 million) over the same period.

Additional research studies also highlight a growing level of regional imbalance within the country as a whole. Many tourists are entering Ireland via Dublin and staying either in the eastern or south-western regions of the country. According to Donegal County Council, it is estimated that only 6 per cent of overseas visitors to Ireland visited the north-west region, and between 1998 and 2003 visitor numbers to the county fell by approximately 30 per cent (Donegal County Council, 2005).

It is envisaged that tourism will continue to play an important role in the Donegal economy, both in generating revenue and in providing employment. On the positive side, Inishowen, for example, is one of the twenty-five areas identified by Fáilte Ireland as having special potential for rural tourism. Tourism products and amenities are reasonably well developed, while the Inishowen Tourism Co-operative is one of the fourteen local community members of the National Rural Community Tourism Co-operative providing a central marketing service while also assuming responsibility for the coordination of rural tourism at a national level.

VENTURE DEVELOPMENT

With a total budget of IR£1,800 (€2,286) from his savings, Pat set about restoring the family home, renovating a barn and developing an outdoor famine exhibition. He completed most of the construction work himself, even making the furniture required for the teahouse and the exhibitions. Previous experience as a set designer for the locally shot film *High Boot Benny* provided Pat with the basic skills he needed for such work.

His first summer season saw approximately 1,000 visitors come to the Centre. Income was derived from a IR£2.50 (€3.17) per head entry fee with additional revenue from the teashop. Pat's first year in business allowed him to test-market his ideas and to find out what visitors were really interested in at a minimal investment cost.

In the months that followed Pat set about developing his vision for a visitor centre further. He researched and collected local folklore and history. He applied for grant aid from the Inishowen Rural Development Agency (IRDL) and was awarded IR£1,800 (€2,286) to develop the project further. He also secured a IR£3,000 (€3,809) bank loan. With a limited level of funding available, he salvaged old wood and materials for use in the development of the Centre.

Through interaction with visitors, Pat began to realise that his interpretation of local history was one-sided and based on the Irish Catholic history that he had been taught at school. In order to create a more balanced approach to how the Centre was presenting and interpreting local history, he held a Famine dinner and invited representatives from all the local churches who, over the course of an evening, discussed how the Famine impacted on their respective congregations. With local musicians providing the entertainment, and potatoes and salt on the menu, a very entertaining night was enjoyed by the 200–300 visitors who attended. This experience initiated a turning point in the historical interpretation of the Centre (see Exhibit 2.1).

In 1999 Pat decided to build a new teahouse, as the existing one was too small. With an additional bank loan of IR£3,000–IR£4,000

Exhibit 2.1
Product Offering – Doagh Famine Village

- Guided tours around the Village
- An Irish Wake
- Presbyterian Meeting House
- An Orange Hall
- A Mass Rock
- An exhibition on the Travelling Community
- Tea House
- Souvenir Shop

A number of events are also held through the summer season, including:

- Traditional Irish Nights and Story Telling
- An Irish Wake and Funeral
- Speed Dating and Matchmaking

Source: http://www.doaghfaminevillage.com/

(€3,809–€5,079) and his own labour, Pat built a substantially bigger tea-house, which could also be used as a multi-purpose space.

FURTHER DEVELOPMENT – THE BIRTH OF DONEGAL'S LAPLAND: SANTA'S ISLAND

While building a wooden chimney in a bid to cut costs, one of Pat's nephews asked why the chimney was so big. In response he was told it was to let Santa Claus down. The idea for Lapland was born.

Lapland was opened in 1999 (see Exhibit 2.2) using the existing cottages and buildings on site and enabled the season to be extended beyond the Easter to September summer season. Starting with a basic concept initially, a Christmas Grotto was created featuring a local farmer's deer and, of course, Santa. Now the concept boasts Santa's Village where you can visit his home, personally place a Christmas order at Santa's office, post your letter in his post office, visit the toy factory and sit on Santa's sleigh. Then you can continue on into the Elves' Kingdom, a different world full of castles, toy factories and an Elf Village. A visit starts with the story of Christmas told by an Elf. Santa always knows each child by name and presents him or her with a present after he pops down the chimney!

Exhibit 2.2
Product Offering – Donegal's Lapland, Santa's Island

Attractions available consist of the Santa's Village and include:

- Theatre where the story of Christmas is told
- Santa's House
- Santa's Office
- Santa's Shops
- Post Office
- Toy Factory
- The Elves' Kingdom, which includes castles, toy factories, village, etc.

Source: http://www.doaghfaminevillage.com/

Lapland runs from the end of November until Christmas Eve. Shows run hourly and the Centre is open seven days a week over this period. With new features being added each year to sustain visitor interest, numbers have grown from 2,000–3,000 in 1999 to approximately 20,000 visitors in 2005, with visitors coming from throughout the island of Ireland.

MARKETING

The Centre was largely promoted via roadside signage designed and made by Pat, as well as brochures and advertisements in the local press and radio. In the early days of the business Pat spent two nights per week depositing brochures around other tourism amenity providers in the north-west region and beyond. In the course of this activity he began to meet and network with other tourism providers. Not only did he learn a lot from this interaction but he also set up a joint venture with Eddie Gallagher, who operates a hostel and pony-trekking business in Ballybofey, Co. Donegal.

The Herrema Connection

Pat realised that he needed to do something dramatic to boost his visitor numbers. Eddie Gallagher was infamous due to his connection with the IRA kidnapping of the Dutch industrialist Dr Tiede Herrema in the 1970s. Pat's plans would enable him not only to expand his product offering through the provision of pony-trekking on local beaches but would also provide a great publicity opportunity. However, when he discussed his plans with other local tourism providers he encountered a lot of opposition. Many feared that such an association could lead to a negative perception of the area and have an adverse effect on their businesses. Faced with a need to substantially improve his visitor numbers to remain in business, Pat made the controversial decision to commence the venture.

While the arrival of Eddie Gallagher and his ponies increased business to some extent and brought a higher volume of visitors to the area, the majority of them were not coming into the Centre. Thus, visitor numbers were still not growing sufficiently. Pat decided to contact the national press. As a result, the *Sunday World* did a two-page feature on Eddie and his association with the Centre. UTV even used the story as a leading headline on the 6 o'clock evening news. The Centre and the area began to receive a lot of positive publicity. These events heralded a major turning point for the business. Visitor numbers doubled as a result with the majority of visitors coming from across the Border.

Due to Eddie Gallagher's association with the Centre a lot of visitors with a Republican perspective started visiting the Centre. In a bid to appeal equally to both sides of the community and broaden his market, Pat decided to develop an Orange Hall exhibition that would trace the local history of the Protestant community. To test the market a miniature version of the Hall was first created. Pat's tourism peers considered this as another controversial move and again he faced opposition locally. In the process of researching for this exhibition, Pat met with the Apprentice Boys of Derry and also some of their representatives in Lurgan. They were both surprised by and supportive of Pat's plans. He discovered that many of them had never been to Inishowen and were wary of visiting the area. These visits were very informative for Pat and he was also gifted with some memorabilia for his new exhibition. As a result of this interaction and further contact with church groups, visitor numbers from this section of the community have increased dramatically.

Group marketing with the local hotels, which offer 'Santa Packages' via brochures and advertisements in the national press, have been very successful and have resulted in increased visitor stays in the area at a normally quiet period of the year. A laser was also installed which beams a ray of light into the night sky over the duration of the Lapland season. This can be seen for miles around and has become a talking point with many people, particularly visitors new to the area, mistaking its effect for the Northern Lights, which can occasionally be seen from this part of the country.

Target Market

The most prevalent visitors to the Centre come from Northern Ireland, followed equally by visitors from Britain and the Republic of Ireland. American visitors would be the next most popular visitor group and their numbers have increased recently due to the introduction of a Belfast–New York flight from Belfast International Airport in Antrim. The French are the next most popular visitor group. The Centre is recommended in a number of guidebooks, such as *Lonely Planet* and some of the French guidebooks.

Employment

Three people are employed full-time in the Centre over the summer season while thirty-five are employed over the Lapland season.

START-UP CHALLENGES

The major challenges that Pat faced in developing his business could be summarised as follows:

Funding and Supports

The Centre was developed on a shoestring and was predominately funded by Pat's own funds and bank loans. A very small amount of grant aid was secured from IRDL, a local development agency. Pat secured a place on the Back to Work Scheme: a government programme designed to assist those on welfare benefits to get back to work, administered locally by the Inishowen Partnership Company. The programme enabled Pat to keep his social welfare benefits on a reducing basis for three years while he developed his business. It also provided him with start-up mentoring and training. This programme was a tremendous help to Pat as it provided him with a basic, but guaranteed, income over this critical start-up period, as well as additional supports.

Location

While the geographical location of the Centre has added to its poignancy, it is remote and difficult to reach. The geographical isolation of Inishowen has resulted in poorer tourism visitor numbers in comparison to the more accessible areas of the rest of the country. The area's isolation has also been exacerbated by a poor road infrastructure and low levels of state transport services in the region. Inishowen's economic and social development has traditionally been hampered by the Troubles in Northern Ireland and its proximity to the Border. With Northern Ireland being one of the main access points to Inishowen, many tourists were wary of travelling through the province to get here. This again gave a negative perception of the area. However, the Good Friday Agreement and the continued ceasefire have improved the overall image of the north-west region and have given tourists a greater sense of security. In addition, the existence of visitor attractions such as the Centre, and improved transportation links to the region, have given visitors a greater impetus to visit the area in recent years.

Transportation Infrastructure, Communications and Access

One of the most important aspects relating to tourism development in County Donegal is the access into, from and around the county. The provision of adequate transport, signage and related facilities within the county is a major issue for visitors to Inishowen and Donegal in general. For example, Doagh Isle does not appear on all maps of the region. In addition, while Doagh Isle is more commonly known as the Isle of Doagh, where it does appear on a map it is usually called Doagh Isle. Thus this version of the name has been selected to appear on all promotional materials in order to avoid confusion.

Road conditions are poor in particular and due to their narrowness roads are not well suited to bus traffic. In addition, due to the occurrence of a number of fatal road accidents recently, Inishowen is developing a reputation as one of the worst road accident black spots in Ireland. As a result, the national speed limit throughout Inishowen was reduced by the government to fifty miles per hour (eighty kilometres per hour) in a bid to reduce the incident of road accidents. This represents a very negative perception for tourism development.

The Weather

This is Ireland and weather will always be an issue with all four seasons in a day definitely possible. Originally part of the exhibition was outside; Pat has now created a weatherproof exhibition area and, thus, improved the attractiveness of a visit to the Centre as an all-weather destination.

A Home-Grown Feel

As mentioned earlier, Pat has designed and built all of the exhibitions himself as well as the majority of the Centre's facilities. There is a homemade and rustic feel to many of the exhibitions. While this gives the Centre a quaintness overall, much more could be done to improve the packaging, presentation and interactivity of some of the exhibitions.

A Family Affair

Pat's business is very much a family one. His extended family helps with the running of the Centre and his wife is one of the tour guides. Despite this, Pat does not appear to have considered the issue of succession and the future strategic development of the Centre. With a young child at home, hopefully Pat will give this issue more thought in the very near future.

FINAL THOUGHTS

Pat's decision to set up a business was based very much on necessity and a "gut feeling" rather than a solid business plan. His feasibility study consisted largely of what he saw and experienced as he travelled the length and breadth of Ireland. Pat's business has grown organically in response to customer demand and available funding.

An early school-leaver with no formal business training, Pat has responded intuitively to the challenges he has faced, and in the process, has demonstrated great entrepreneurial flair. He is a born entrepreneur. Pat is driven by a passion for this unique part of Ireland, by a yearning to live and work on the land of his birth and by a desire to make a difference!

Pat would appear to have many of the characteristics often cited as necessary for being a successful entrepreneur. He is resourceful, a creative and innovative problem-solver, hard working, self-disciplined, confident, a risk-taker and obsessively opportunity-focused. He has shown an unrelenting determination, despite many challenges, to achieve his entrepreneurial objectives; essential ingredients probably for prospering in an area that has remained untouched by the "Celtic Tiger", a popular euphemism for Ireland's economic miracle. However, while Pat still faces a number of challenges, the Doagh Isle Visitor Centre is a miracle in itself – proof of what can be achieved with an entrepreneurial mindset, self-belief and a lot of hard work.

References

Donegal County Council, Draft Development Plan 2005.

Fáilte Ireland, *Strategy Statement 2005–2007*, available at: http://www.failteireland.ie/upload/documents/Failte%20Ireland%20Strategy%20Statement%202005%20-%202007.doc, 2005.

Inishowen Partnership Co, Local Development Plan 2000–2003.

Inish Times, Vol. 7, Issue 43, 17 May 2005.

Tourism Action Plan Implementation Group, Third and Final Report to Minister for Arts, Sport and Tourism, March 2006.

NOTES

1. Sharon Porter is a Teaching Fellow in Entrepreneurship with the Northern Ireland Centre for Entrepreneurship (NICENT) at the University of Ulster. Email: s.porter@ulster.ac.uk
2. This case was written as a basis for class discussion rather than to illustrate either effective or ineffective handling of an administrative situation.

THE MORGAN INSTITUTE[1]

BREDA O'DWYER AND ANN SEARS[2]

As Brenda Morgan, founder of the Morgan Institute, was finishing up a radio interview with Radio Kerry, she was pondering about the change in direction the company had taken since her first radio interview in February 2005. As she left the Radio Kerry building she could not help but feel a little bit unnerved and uneasy. She kept repeating her last statement to the interviewer over and over in her head: "I could never have planned or hoped for this level of success so soon. It all just happened!" Suddenly her mobile rings. It is the manager of the Genesis Enterprise Programme congratulating her on a successful interview with Radio Kerry, who had asked the very same question that was bothering Brenda. Why did it all just happen? More to the point, how would she be able to sustain and build on this success in the future? The manager reminded Brenda that the answer was needed in the marketing plan that was due for submission the following week! Reality dawned. Brenda had one week to mature in the business planning world. Brenda had plans and strategies to formulate for the future of the business. Growth decisions needed to be made, of that she was sure, but which markets to target was yet to be decided.

IDEA DEVELOPMENT

Brenda trained as a teacher, obtained her H.Dip. and taught in second-level education for ten years before starting her own business in the summer of 2003. After eight years of teaching in a temporary position she realised that there was no possibility of her job becoming permanent, so she started

29

thinking of other possibilities for her future. Parallel to this Brenda became disillusioned with her teacher training:

> I realised that with all my teacher training none of my training showed me how to teach students to study and how to learn.

Brenda recognised a gap in the market – students in second level did not know how to study and how to learn. She wanted to start a mission to change that phenomenon; she called it her "student mission". Brenda decided that she would "up skill" to get the necessary training that would help her to help her students. However, such training did not exist in Ireland. In April 2003, she trained as a 'PhotoReading Instructor', which is the pinnacle of Accelerated and Advanced Learning and the basis of her business idea.

THE START-UP PHASE

In the first year of business Brenda developed a full-time evening support programme for fifth and sixth year students. This was launched in September 2003 and was available in two locations, Tralee and Killarney. Brenda chose those locations based solely on convenience. She was still teaching full-time in Killarney and she lived in Tralee.

> I began with 17 students in Killarney and 5 in Tralee. I was advised (by family and friends) not to run with Tralee, but I was stubborn and knew that it would take off. I had done a lot of groundwork in Killarney but not in Tralee.

At that time, Brenda had no business training or business experience. Marketing efforts were almost non-existent, promotional efforts were based on word-of-mouth, no pricing strategy was in place and competitors were unknown. Since Brenda was "naively" unaware of competition, she was, therefore, unable to use these as a benchmark or a positioning tool. Her financial advisor was worried by this fact and suggested the need for competitive analysis. However, there was no time to conduct this analysis. The academic year was about to start and, therefore, it was necessary to identify a price sooner rather than later. It was agreed to charge each student €2.50 per hour and the course began in September 2003.

Time was spent on designing the product and it was developed from the customer's perspective. This process was not a problem to Brenda – after all she had personal inside knowledge of the educational sector.

The Study Manager programme was developed to include the following:

1. A small supportive, positive study group.
2. Active supervision (a teacher present to help with homework).
3. Study plans designed for the students in each of their subjects.
4. Study deadlines – students had to produce work monthly.
5. Regular progress reports for parents.
6. Training in how to approach study in a brain-friendly way.
7. A 32-week programme: Monday to Thursday, 5 p.m.–9 p.m.

Source: Morgan Institute website (http://www.morganinstitute.com)

The business idea was accepted by the target market and the two locations achieved full capacity. The idea was a success; a business was born. However, despite the positive reaction to the product, Brenda was not prepared for the business opportunities created by her idea. It became clear that she needed to gain knowledge in business areas such as business advice, support, finance, etc. In that first year, seven teachers were employed to help run the programme and her sister Una was taken on to do the accounts for the business. Brenda received advice from the Kerry Enterprise Board who gave her a grant of 50 per cent of her start-up costs, which Brenda estimated at €9,000.

She became part of the Genesis Enterprise Programme (GEP)[3] in April 2004 and, through this programme, she wrote up a business plan. This programme provided Brenda with access to mentors and business advisors who, at that time, suggested that she should consider franchising the business idea. Brenda was not keen on this recommendation. She felt it was better to understand the intricacies of the product before franchising the idea to others.

THE GROWTH PHASE IN YEAR TWO

The second year of the business started without any external funding. Brenda dedicated herself full-time to the development of her business idea. She expanded the customer base to include second and third year students, branding it the Junior Programme. However, the product was not modified to suit the particular needs of this type of student. Essentially, the same programme was being offered to two different customer segments. It was quickly recognised that the needs of the Junior Programme students were vastly different to those in the original programme (now known as the Senior Programme), and adjustments were made to the product offering accordingly.

Year Two of the business witnessed many changes. During this time, Brenda decided to obtain a Masters in Education, which she completed in one year at UCC. Her thesis was entitled '21st Century Teaching Methods for 21st Century Students'. During this year the company moved from their home-based office to the Tom Crean Business Centre located on the campus of the Institute of Technology, Tralee. The business won 'Best Progress Made to Date' award from Genesis and received favourable radio and print coverage as a result. Additional changes were to be experienced due to entering new markets.

Up to this point, the business had focused solely on the student market. However, as a result of radio interviews, businesses and government departments started making contact, requesting training in the products that were offered by the company. This was something that Brenda had not envisioned at the start of the business but it was such an important opportunity that it could not be ignored. As Brenda recalled:

In April 2005, I did two introductory sessions for the staff in the Department of Communication, Marine and Natural Resources and the feedback was incredible. They wanted everything that I could offer them! They were only one of many, many calls. The business was taking on a life of its own and I was not in a position to run with it. I was still out four nights a week with my students and trying to juggle this new interest too.

Brenda began to wonder what she had created and how she could manage the evolution of her creation.

Consciously or subconsciously, Brenda had, in the interim, applied the international transfer concept to her business. She had introduced and delivered the 'PhotoReading'[4] model to the Irish market. She had strategically aligned herself with an American company known as Learning Strategies Corporation (www.learningstrategies.com). This company was founded in 1981 as a consulting and training company. It has evolved into a premier provider of self-improvement, education and health programmes. One of the co-founders, Paul Scheele, offers significant expertise in the following areas:

- Neuro-Linguistic Programming (NLP), which imparts a unique understanding of how the human brain works.
- Accelerated Learning, which provides keys to learning five to fifty times faster than traditional techniques.
- Preconscious Processing, which gives access to the vast capacity of the mind to accomplish virtually anything.

The strategic alignment with Learning Strategies Corporation was a win-win for all involved. The Learning Strategies Corporation wanted access to the European market and The Morgan Institute wanted an accredited product for the corporate sector. PhotoReading enables one to:

- Read more easily with better understanding.
- Improve memory and sharpen concentration.
- Increase productivity.
- Enhance intuition and develop true potential.
- Read at speeds of up to 25,000 words a minute.
- Catapult oneself into a bright future.

Source: Morgan Institute website (http://www.morganinstitute.com)

Paul Scheele, Chairman of Learning Strategies Corporation, commented:

> Brenda Morgan is one of the most enthusiastic and committed people I know. She represents the highest level of professionalism and integrity in a field of critical importance today: whole-person teaching and learning (http://www.morganinstitute.com/photoreading.html).

The success of the business to date was most certainly underpinned by the passion and vision of its owner.

CHANGES MADE IN YEAR THREE

Over the past year, The Morgan Institute has received positive publicity from airtime on the Sunday Business Show on Today FM and Radio

Kerry. New markets have emerged for the company as a direct result of those interviews. As the third year of the business started, Brenda, together with her mentor and financial advisor, decided to roll-out the Study Manger Programme in Cork and Dublin. Indirectly, they decided to re-brand the product and called it 'The Advanced Study Programme'. "All was great", said Brenda. The company was expanding with little or no investment.

Over the summer, instructors were brought in from the USA to train twenty-seven teachers in preparation for the year ahead. The original seven teachers, together with Brenda, could not sustain the growth of the business. The plan was to wait until the Leaving Certificate results were released and to launch their new product in the new locations.

Despite an inherent knowledge of the educational sector, the business did not receive any marketing advice. The financial advisor and the mentor did not realise the importance or the need for marketing. The only planned marketing efforts were in relation to the promotional campaign for Cork and Dublin. This involved the making of a flyer and the distribution of same to households in those locations. Surely this would be enough and business would be booming as a result of their promotional efforts. After all, this would simply replicate what happened in the past in Killarney and Tralee. However, this assumption was far from reality. The fact that no one received their flyers was unknown to The Morgan Institute for some time. Unfortunately, this was due to an unforeseen postal strike, which was outside of their control. The limited marketing budget was spent on the flyers and they found themselves in a dilemma. The Kerry locations were running at full capacity and were funding the Dublin and Cork centres. The school year was progressing and the customers did not materialise in the new locations. Brenda had to make tough decisions regarding the new locations and the next step for the business. She decided to pull back on the roll-out strategy and learn from the mistake of geographic expansion too fast, too soon. One may also attribute this mistake to the lack of business experience.

Brenda was certain of one thing – action was needed. Her learning curve was put into 'top gear' as she had to learn about marketing and finance fast and how to apply these concepts to keep her company in business. Money was tight and this would have an impact on promotion within the school sector. Brenda had realised that, because schools were able to make a significant profit from evening study, they perceived her as a direct form of competition. This, she believed, was the root of the lack of proactive cooperation from the schools.

Although she did not realise it, she decided to adopt a 'pull strategy'. She contacted the schools in early October/November 2005 with regards to providing the students with information on the 'Advanced Learning Programme'. The response was amazing. Schools were calling her from all over the country, asking her to present the talk to their students. They were delighted with the opportunity of an alternative supplier to the one existing competitor – Student Enrichment Services. Teachers wanted to know more about the product offering, particularly any training that might be of benefit to them. The positive effect of the free form of 'word-of-mouth' had been realised for The Morgan Institute. Brenda was beginning to get the hang of the promotional concept. She would go to a school and spend a day training students in groups of between thirty and fifty students, for an individual fee of €25.00 per student for this one session. But more importantly, each student was asked to fill in a form with their name and address. Brenda had initiated and generated her first database of students, which could now be used for direct marketing purposes. The school market had opened the floodgates, again. This had generated the need to consider other products and other markets. Brenda needed to decide which way to expand the business and whether she should grow the business through product development, through market development or both.

A list of the possible programmes and training available from The Morgan Institute are contained in the appendices.

BRENDA THE ENTREPRENEUR

Brenda has the classic entrepreneurial characteristics: she is enthusiastic, passionate, motivated, determined, hard-working, committed to people, able to communicate her vision for the business and has self-belief in what she is doing. She has all this and still manages to function as a wife and mother to her four young children. In the past she has commented that:

> Not once did I doubt what we were doing. Not once did the thought of returning to teaching enter my mind. Not once did I seriously consider failure as an option.

However, Brenda's background does not point in the entrepreneurial direction. Her mother was a homemaker, raising five children, and her father was a company manager. None of her siblings went down the self-employment route. Her sister Una is her accountant and another sister may start working for the Morgan Institute in the near future. The involvement of the second sister may be in the area of product development, particularly in the area of kinesiology. The support of her siblings may be regarded as the seed of the first generation of a family business.

THE FUTURE OF THE BUSINESS

The Morgan Institute is Brenda's first entrepreneurial venture. She is successful but still unsure as to the origin of her entrepreneurial tendencies. The source may be found in the frustration of her own career and her need to do something different. The question remains, is Brenda an entrepreneur because of nature or nurture – or is it a combination of both? Did she become self-employed due to the frustration of her own career? Does the entrepreneur need to be intimate with their own business, or can they outsource some of the key functions, e.g. finance and marketing? In the case of The Morgan Institute, what are the particular implications of outsourcing for the future of the business?

As Brenda got into her car after the Radio Kerry interview she felt hopeful and enthusiastic for the future. As she drove back to the office after the interview she started to give some thought to how the past had "just happened". Maybe it did not "just happen" but had been supported through informal planning. She now needed to formalise that planning process for the future viability of the business. One option may be to penetrate the education sector in the primary, secondary and third level sectors by promoting one product. Another option may be to expand the market into the business sector. Yet another option maybe to offer more than one product to different markets. For example, training supervisors in the business sector on PhotoReading techniques, which they could then deliver to their staff. She had a number of options; it was simply a matter of choosing the most effective strategy for the long-term viability of the business. She felt well supported, with self-acquired business skills and access to many more. But what would be the right way to go and why? Maybe she did not know the answer to this, but Brenda knew one thing for sure – she was determined to make it work and, this time, she would plan the growth.

Interview

Morgan, Brenda (2006): Director of the Morgan Institute, interview via email, 27 January 2006.

NOTES

1. This case was written as a basis for class discussion rather than to illustrate either effective or ineffective handling of an administrative situation.
2. Breda O'Dwyer and Ann Sears lecture at the Institute of Technology, Tralee.
3. The GEP is a 12-month, rapid incubation programme that aims to support and accelerate graduate entrepreneurs in developing a business from a very early stage. Candidates may participate on the GEP if they have an innovative idea with export potential and are looking to develop that potential into a business. It is specifically targeted at graduates who have already gained several years of experience in the work place and are now aiming to start their own business. Candidates must have earned a third level qualification in order to be eligible to apply. Further information is available from www.gep.ie.
4. See www.learningstrategies.com/PhotoReading/Home.asp for further information.

Appendix 3.1: **Primary School Training**

Teachers
Advanced Teaching Methodology
Advanced Learning for Younger Children
PhotoReading
'Teacher Talk' – Connect with your students and build rapport
Health and Energy – This training is run in conjunction with Applied Kinesiology Ireland
1-2-3 Teacher Magic – The Ultimate 'Win-Win' Discipline Approach
'Stay Aware, Stay Safe'

Parents
'Understanding Your Child at School' – Advanced Study & Learning Training
Parent Magic – 1-2-3 Magic Programme for parents of children 2–12 years
Health and Energy
PhotoReading
Parent Talk – Connect with your children and build rapport
'Stay Aware, Stay Safe'

Source: Morgan Institute website (http://www.morganinstitute.com)

Appendix 3.2: **Second Level Training**

Students
Advanced Study and Learning
Exam-Taking Strategies
Three-Day Option: Exam year students are supported throughout the year

- September: Advanced Study and Learning
- January: Exam-Taking Strategies
- Easter: 'Through the Roof' Productivity

'Smooth Secondary School' – Training for First Year students to help them settle into Secondary School Life
Transition Year Fun

- Creativity and Imagination
- The Ultimate Life Plan for Teens
- Play with Your Genius Mind

The Advanced Study Programme
'Stay Aware, Stay Safe'

Teachers
Advanced Teaching Methodology
Advanced Study and Learning
PhotoReading
'Teacher Talk' – Connect with your students and build rapport
The Ultimate Life Plan for Educators
Health and Energy – This training is run in conjunction with Applied Kinesiology Ireland
Teacher Magic – The Ultimate 'Win-Win' Discipline Approach
'Stay Aware, Stay Safe'

Parents
'Understanding Your Teen at School' – Advanced Study & Learning Training
Parent Magic – 'Surviving Your Adolescent' Programme for parents of teens
Health and Energy
PhotoReading
The Ultimate Life Plan for Parents

Parent Talk – Connect with your teens and build rapport
'Stay Aware, Stay Safe'

Source: Morgan Institute website (http://www.morganinstitute.com)

Appendix 3.3: **Third Level Training**

Students
Advanced Study and Learning
Exam Taking Strategies
PhotoReading
'How Not to Fail First Year in College' – Total orientation for First Year Students
The Ultimate Life Plan for Students
'Stay Aware, Stay Safe' – This training is run in conjunction with John Brawn who specialises in Self Awareness & Self Protection Programmes (Rather than 'Self Defence' per se)

Lecturers
Advanced Teaching Methodology
Advanced Study and Learning
PhotoReading
'Teacher Talk' – connect with your students and build rapport
Health and Energy – This training is run in conjunction with Applied Kinesiology Ireland
The Ultimate Life Plan for Educators
Parent Magic – because Lecturers are parents too!
'Stay Aware, Stay Safe'

Source: Morgan Institute website (http://www.morganinstitute.com)

Appendix 3.4: **Corporate & Business Training**

Advanced Study and Learning
PhotoReading
'People Talk' – Connect with your colleagues and clients to build rapport
Health and Energy – This training is run in conjunction with Applied Kinesiology Ireland
The Ultimate Life Plan for Busy People
Parent Magic
Play With Your Genius Mind
'Stay Aware, Stay Safe'

Source: Morgan Institute website (http://www.morganinstitute.com)

GUARDIAN ANGEL[1]

THOMAS M. COONEY[2]

It was the summer of 2006 and three friends of many years had come up with a business idea that they believed could be a money-spinner for all of them. Maria Harrison, Krystle Malone and Marie Lyons had all been students at the Dublin Institute of Technology and had recently completed their degree in Marketing. As part of their programme they had taken a course on Entrepreneurship by way of interest rather than any deep-rooted desire to start their own business. But now, they are about to meet a venture capital company to ask for €300,000 to get the business started. They would never have dreamed, as they walked into their first class on entrepreneurship, that six months later they would be in this position.

As part of the coursework in the Entrepreneurship class, students were asked to develop a business opportunity and to write a Business Plan to evaluate that opportunity. Maria, Krystle and Marie spent a great deal of time brainstorming for a business opportunity but none of the ideas generated appealed to them. Indeed, it felt like the harder they worked, the less attractive the business ideas became. One night, after many more hours of fruitless effort, they needed to take a break and so went to the kitchen to have a coffee. In the background, a television was disturbing the peace that they needed to concentrate and, as Marie went to turn it off, an advertisement appeared showing the threat posed by carbon monoxide in the home. By way of conversation, Marie mentioned the advertisement to Maria and Krystle, who both commented on an article that they had recently read for another class in college on the number of people who die each year in their homes from smoke inhalation and from gas leaks. "Wouldn't it be great if there was something that acted as an alarm for all three of them at the same time?" said Marie. Maria and Krystle looked at her as if she had suddenly won the lottery. "That's it!" they shouted, almost in unison, "that's our business idea, a single alarm system that caters for all three dangers. Now all we need to do is write the Business Plan!!"

Over the three months that followed, the three friends spent a large amount of their time working on this project, frequently to the detriment of their course work for other classes. Eventually they completed the plan and quite proudly submitted it to their lecturer. Indeed, the plan was so good that they presented the same one to a venture capitalist two months later, but this time it was for real!

As they sat waiting in the reception area of the venture capital company, the three friends began to wonder how they managed to get this far so quickly. They started to think about their business plan and whether it would be robust enough for the venture capitalists. Was there enough detail? Would the figures stand up? Suddenly, the door opened and a polite voice said, "Sorry for keeping you. They are ready for you now. Please come in." This was it. Had they done all their homework? They were about to find out!

THE BUSINESS PLAN FOR 'GUARDIAN ANGEL'

EXECUTIVE SUMMARY

- Guardian Angel is a combined natural gas, carbon monoxide (CO) and smoke detection system.
- Guardian Angel is cube-shaped, approximately five inches in width, four inches in length and two inches in breadth. The face of the unit has a reset button, a speaker and a digital LED display.
- The product is light, weighing approximately 200 grams. It is battery operated using a 9V battery and it also incorporates a battery failure alert.
- The circuit board is manufactured to meet ISO 9000 standards and to meet UL BS9000 and UL 796 standards. The finished product will meet all CE standards.
- The primary goal of the company is to become the market leader in the domestic gas and smoke detection market in Ireland by the end of Year One.
- The key market trends for natural gas, CO and smoke detection are all highly favourable.
- The success of the company will be based on the organisation's ability to effectively communicate the need for this product to its target audience through its marketing campaign.
- The firm's primary research segmented the Irish market and identified two core target markets, which are the "grey" market and family households with children.
- No other three-in-one carbon monoxide, natural gas and smoke detection systems are available in hardware stores in Ireland.
- The Gas Maestro (Canadian product) is only available in one outlet in Ireland, through a family-run business in Co. Kildare.
- The company has opted to sell Guardian Angel at a price lower than direct and indirect competitors.
- The company will distribute Guardian Angel throughout the fifty locations of the four main hardware stores in Ireland. It will also be available through the Internet.
- The company is going to opt for shock advertisement as the theme for the marketing campaign using a variety of different media.

- The company will outsource the production of all parts to a number of different suppliers.
- A minimum of €300,000 is required in order to establish Saviour Life Ltd.
- The accounts foresee the company turning over a profit of €16,045 in Year Two and €145,761 in Year Three.

MANAGEMENT

Introduction

The idea for Saviour Life Limited was developed in 2005 by Marie Lyons, Maria Harrison and Krystle Malone. The company will go into operation on 1 January 2007. The business idea was developed when an awareness campaign regarding the dangers of carbon monoxide (CO) in the home was launched in 2004. This campaign brought to the management team's attention a hazardous problem which has the potential to exist in every building in Ireland. Concurrently running were safety campaigns regarding the safe use of natural gas in the home and fire safety. The management team sought out a three-in-one solution for these dangers in the home and found that, unless the Internet was used, a solution was not easily available for purchase in Ireland. The company consulted with an engineering advisor who confirmed it would be possible to manufacture such a product in Ireland. After conducting research the decision was made to produce a three-in-one natural gas, CO and smoke detection system. The name Guardian Angel was chosen for the detection system because other firms producing this product have chosen to use informative and scientific names such as Gas Maestro. In contrast to this, Guardian Angel is making an emotional, yet informative appeal to its target audience. The product will act like a guardian angel over the premises into which it is installed.

Business Objectives:

- To establish the Guardian Angel brand as a household name by the end of Year One.
- To become market leader in the domestic gas and smoke detection market in Ireland by the end of Year One.
- To reach sales of 15,132 units in Year One, 26,093 units in Year Two and 33,853 units in Year Three.

- To promote innovation within the company and have a new home safety product ready for the market by the end of Year Four.

Mission Statement

The mission for Saviour Life Ltd. is "to manufacture new creative safety products for the home to the highest standards possible to meet the needs of its customers and to create superior value for all stakeholders".

Organisational Structure

Saviour Life Ltd. is to be registered as a private limited company. A registered company is recognised in law as a legal person independent of its members. This means that all members in the firm have limited liability. The benefits of a private limited company also include the fact that the firm can raise additional finance by the issuing of shares. Saviour Life Ltd. will have six employees in Year One: three directors, one quality control technician and two operatives. A third operative will be hired in Year Two. The founders Marie Lyons, Maria Harrison and Krystle Malone will make up the Board of Directors in the company. Each director will be in charge of a number of duties within the firm. A Board of Directors meeting will be held once every two weeks for the first year in business to share information and evaluate how each section of the firm is operating. If at the end of the first year the business is operating smoothly and each section of the firm is running in conjunction with the others, then the Board of Directors meetings will be held every month.

Maria Harrison will be in charge of dealing with clientele (such as retail stores). One of her major responsibilities will be to build good customer relationships with the clients and to secure sales. Maria will also be the Managing Director.

Krystle Malone will organise the accounts for the firm. A registered accountant will be hired to prepare the accounts and it will be Ms. Malone's responsibility to liaise with the accountant. When a regular turnover becomes established she will hire a full time professional accountant. Ms. Malone will be responsible for ensuring that all debts are collected on time and that all creditors are paid promptly. She will be in charge of presenting financial statements at every Board of Directors meeting. She will also be accountable for ensuring that all staff wages are correct and paid on time.

Marie Lyons will be in charge of deliveries, which will involve distributing the products to retailers and maintaining appropriate stock levels. Her responsibilities will include ensuring there is enough of each material required for the product available to meet stock orders and that stock orders are filled on time without delay.

Operatives will require no prior experience or qualifications. The **Quality Control Technician** (QCT) will supervise the operatives each day. They will also be responsible for training in new operatives and inspecting input components and batches of the completed products. The QCT will require a relevant qualification such as a degree in electrical and control engineering. **Key Advisors** will be appointed, such as a registered accountant who will view the accounts on a regular basis, a solicitor who will provide legal services when necessary and an engineer who will be the company's operations advisor.

SWOT Analysis

Through extensive research the strengths, weaknesses, opportunities and threats to Saviour Life Ltd. have been identified and are listed in Exhibit 4.1.

PRODUCT DESCRIPTION

Guardian Angel is a combined natural gas, CO and smoke detection system. An alarm will sound if any of these toxic fumes are present in the air at dangerous levels. **The sensors** in the Guardian Angel have an operating range of $-40°$ C to $55°$ C. This is more than sufficient for the domestic market (where normal temperature is $22°$ C). The **natural gas** detection sensor will sound an alarm when the concentration of gas in the surrounding air reaches the 5 per cent lowest explosion limit. When the alarm sounds the digital LED display will flash "GAS". The **smoke** detector has an ionization-type sensor. Ionization detectors respond to *invisible* by-products of combustion. They operate by sensing a change in the electrical conductivity across the detection chamber. The advantage of the ionization detector is that it will sense smoke even when it is still invisible to the human eye, while photoelectric smoke detectors look for the presence of *visible* by-products of combustion in the detection chamber.

The **CO** detection sensor will sound an alarm if CO is present at a given concentration for a certain period of time. This is determined by a complex formula that mimics the accumulation of CO in the haemoglobin of a person's red blood cells; this calculation is done by an internal microprocessor.

Exhibit 4.1
SWOT Analysis for Saviour Life

Strengths	Weaknesses
• A highly qualified advisory board. • Committed, dedicated and motivated founders. • Three directors with marketing qualifications. • Three directors with extensive work experience in a variety of other firms. • The product is in demand in the Irish domestic market.	• No established brand name. • No market share. • The management team has no experience of running a company. • Only have one initial product.
Opportunities	**Threats**
• CO and natural gas safety awareness campaigns are currently running in Ireland. • Continuous fire safety campaigns are conducted by the National Safety Council (NSC) in Ireland and other television channels available in the country. • No other company is manufacturing this product in Ireland.	• The availability of similar products such as Gas Maestro on the Internet. • The threat of new entrants entering the Irish domestic market, such as Qtronics and selling their products through retail outlets. • The threat that another cheaper and simpler solution to the problems will be produced.

When the alarm sounds the digital LED display will flash "CO". By using three separate sensors to detect the two gases and the smoke, this means the unit boasts 100 per cent sensitivity for the three substances.

Guardian Angel is cube-shaped, approximately five inches in width, four inches in length and two inches in breadth. The face of the unit has a reset button, a speaker and a digital LED display. The reset button allows the user to switch off the alarm when it sounds. The speaker transmits the alarm sound and the digital LED displays information in relation to the cause of the alarm. The product is light, weighing approximately 200 grams. It is battery-operated using a 9V battery and it also incorporates a battery failure alert.

The unit should be installed on to the ceiling or high on a wall. It is mounted by means of a formed aluminium mounting plate. This plate is screwed to the ceiling or wall and the unit can easily slide on and off. This makes the task of changing batteries quick and simple. It is an aesthetically pleasing product which does not "stand out". The plastic casing of the alarm unit will be manufactured from the heat resistant plastic polypropylene (PP). This plastic is currently used in smoke alarm manufacture and is most suited, as it is very robust.

The circuit board is manufactured to meet ISO 9000 standards and to meet UL BS9000 and UL 796 standards. The finished product will meet all CE standards. The Guardian Angel will have a two-year full replacement warranty. It will be packaged in a cardboard box with instructions included inside the box. The firm will be promoting continuous innovation among employees and plans to have a new home safety product ready for the market by the end of Year Four. The engineering advisor will be consulted throughout the innovation process.

TARGET MARKET

Market Information

Natural Gas Trends: Since the establishment of Bord Gáis under the 1976 Gas Act the growth in demand for natural gas has grown year on year. To date the company provides almost half a million households with access to natural gas as well as 16,500 industrial and commercial users (www.bordgais.ie). 90 per cent of households have central heating in Ireland. In urban areas gas has overtaken the use of oil, with 37.8 per cent using gas, compared to 32.5 per cent of households using oil (www.cso.ie). A market segmentation of heating appliances used in Irish homes was conducted in 2002. The results showed that 24.2 per cent (311,696 households) use a gas fire. Research conducted by Media Live show that 33.2 per cent of adults are living in a house with a gas cooker (www.medialive.ie). Natural gas is completely safe when it is sealed inside pipes and used properly. However, leaks can occur and people can forget to turn off gas appliances. If there is a flame lit or a spark in the area of a leak, it could cause an explosion. To combat this problem the gas companies have added a chemical called "mercaptan" to make natural gas smell distinctive. However, this alone is not a sufficient way to deal with the potential risk of gas leaks. Saviour Life Ltd.'s research confirms that people are still highly concerned about the dangers of gas in the home.

Fire Trends: Statistics show that a person is six times more likely to die in a fire if they live in a home without a working smoke alarm (www. nihe.gov.uk). Of the thirty-seven people who lost their lives in the Republic of Ireland in 2003, smoke alarms were only found to be working in two cases. Past research conducted by the National Safety Council (NSC) found that those at greatest risk are the under-12s and over-60s. Deaths caused by fire have fallen slightly in recent years but the NSC fears that they will drastically rise again due to their findings in a recent telephone poll of smokers. The research revealed that 42 per cent of respondents indicated their intention to entertain at home more often as a direct result of the smoking ban enforced by the Irish government. When people consume alcohol the chances of them falling asleep unexpectedly dramatically rise and now, with more smokers consuming alcohol at home, this could result in more people falling asleep while a cigarette is still lit. Most fatal fires occur at night when people are asleep. Working smoke alarms cut the risk of dying in a home fire by 50 per cent. Currently approximately 70 per cent of all households in Ireland have a smoke alarm, which means that 70 per cent of the primary target market is already safety conscious. Through the firm's informative marketing campaign this segment can also be made aware of the hazards of natural gas and carbon monoxide in the home.

Carbon Monoxide Trends: Carbon monoxide is easily produced in the home when appliances burning fossil fuels such as gas, coal or oil do not completely combust. Carbon monoxide is a colourless, odourless, tasteless and toxic gas, and is often referred to as the "silent killer". When inhaled it inhibits the blood's capacity to transport oxygen throughout the body. Early symptoms include flu-like symptoms such as fatigue, weakness, dizziness, nausea and headaches. Advanced symptoms include disorientation, unconsciousness and convulsions, ultimately causing permanent brain damage, mental and speech disorders, hearing impairment, coma or death. A national campaign called "Carbon Monoxide – The Silent Killer" has been launched to inform people in Ireland of the dangers of CO in the home. When the campaign is completed it will be an appropriate time to launch Guardian Angel in Ireland. Saviour Life Ltd. will enter the marketplace offering a solution to this problem.

The success of the company will be based on the organisation's ability to effectively communicate the need for this product to its target audience through its marketing campaign. This will be done by exploiting the company's strengths, which include the management team's marketing skills. Saviour Life Ltd. will be investing €144,000 in Year One and €60,000 in each subsequent year into sales promotions and marketing.

Key Competitors

Similar three-in-one products to Guardian Angel are available overseas. Companies manufacturing these products include Qtronics who produce the **Gas Maestro**. Although Irish customers can order them over the Internet, customers must go on the Internet searching for the product. Since only 537,000 homes in Ireland are connected to the Internet, this means that 750,958 homes have no means of finding out about or buying the products. Potential customers could also use the Internet at work or at Internet cafes to purchase the products but numbers here were more difficult to ascertain for these locations. The Gas Maestro is only available in one outlet in Ireland, **Lowtown Marine Services Ltd.** The firm sells the product for €150. The firm specialises in selling stock required for boats and offers marine services.

Vistec Limited is reputedly Ireland's number one gas detecting company. They target industrial and commercial enterprises, along with government buildings, colleges, hospitals and hotels. **Mac Alarms** was established in Ireland in 1988 and employs over ten engineers. The company provides a comprehensive range of fire detection devices to government and public sector institutions, and commercial and industrial organisations. **Chubb** is the leading provider of security and fire protection services to the business in dustry in the UK and Ireland. All three of the companies mentioned here focus on the industrial and boating market but do not focus on the domestic market. Saviour Life Ltd.'s primary target market will be the domestic market. Indirect competition includes standard smoke alarms and CO alarms. **SafeLincs** provides a range of quality smoke alarms and CO alarms which are manufactured in Ireland. The firm is solely a virtual company and all purchases must be made via the Internet. **Kidde** and **E1** detectors have the largest presence in hardware stores throughout the country but do not offer a three-in-one solution. Saviour Life Ltd. will be offering a three-in-one solution.

Unique Selling Point

The product is easily purchased and easily installed. Guardian Angel will be distributed in hardware stores across the country as well as on Saviour Life Ltd.'s website. No other three-in-one carbon monoxide, natural gas and smoke detection system is available in hardware stores in Ireland.

Market Research

Both quantitative and qualitative primary research was undertaken for the purposes of examining the viability of the business idea. The objectives of the **quantitative research** were:

- To discover if the Irish market is aware of the dangers of natural gas, fire and carbon monoxide within the home.
- To determine the level of concern existing in relation to the dangers of natural gas, fire and carbon monoxide in the Irish marketplace.
- To investigate if there was a market in Ireland for the Guardian Angel.
- To identify the market segments towards which Guardian Angel should be targeted.
- To find out how many people would be willing to purchase the Guardian Angel.

To achieve these objectives the management team created a questionnaire containing ten key questions. As the Guardian Angel is to be launched nationally, a quota sampling was utilised to make the results more representative of the whole country. A minimum of twenty-five respondents were required from both the Dublin suburbs and rural towns. One hundred questionnaires in total were distributed on 24 November 2005. Fifty questionnaires were handed out in Rush town's primary supermarket, twenty-five were handed door to door in south Dublin and twenty-five were handed out door-to-door in Ratoath, Co. Meath. Eighty-four surveys were returned and entered into SPSS for analysis.

The main objective of the **qualitative research** conducted was to develop a foundation for a marketing strategy. An in-depth interview was conducted with a person from each target segment. The interviewees were Jim Murphy, a 29-year-old builder, and Jack Dempsey, a 56-year-old building contractor. Probing techniques were used to reveal their true attitudes and opinions on how Guardian Angel should best be marketed.

Analysis of Quantitative Research

The following are some of the main results from the market research:

- 70 per cent of all respondents are aware of the dangers of CO in the home.
- 83.7 per cent are aware of the dangers of natural gas in the home.
- 86 per cent of respondents are concerned about fire in the home.
- Results highlighted that no correlation exists between gender and concern about CO, natural gas and fire exposure in the home. Therefore a marketing campaign that is not gender specific will be designed.
- The results show that people over fifty years of age and upward are the most concerned about the three potential risks in the home.
- Analysis revealed that the age of people's children was not a determining factor as to whether respondents were concerned about the three toxic fumes in the home. Therefore "age of children" as a contributory factor in segmenting the marketplace was dismissed.
- Of the non-family households that responded, 50 per cent are not concerned with fire, 100 per cent are not concerned with CO and 50 per cent are not concerned with the dangers of natural gas in the home. For this reason non-family households will not be a primary target market.
- Of the couples with children that responded, an average of 75 per cent of this segment was concerned with the dangers of the three toxic fumes in the home. Of the lone parents that responded, on average over 50 per cent were concerned with the dangers of the three toxic fumes in the home. Therefore family units will be one of the primary target markets.
- 82 per cent of respondents confirmed they would purchase a combined natural gas, CO and smoke detection system.

Analysis of Qualitative Research

Throughout the in-depth interviews, it was noted that the type of advertisements with the highest recall were those created by the NSC relating to road deaths in Ireland. The results of the interviews led the management team to opt for shock advertisement as the main theme of Guardian Angel's marketing campaign. Shock advertisement was chosen because representatives of both target segments felt that this form of advertisement is the best way to market a product that protects people against dangers.

One respondent stated that after seeing the latest campaign from the National Road Safety Council, he was distraught. He claimed that:

> You have to be shocked when you see an ad in order for it to really make an impact. You need to look at the ad and think, oh God, imagine if that happened to my family, to my child.

Profile of Target Market

Saviour Life Ltd. will be targeting all 1,287,958 households in the Republic of Ireland. The firm's primary research segmented the Irish market and identified two core target markets. These are **the grey market** and **family households with children**. There are 787,547 people over fifty-five years of age in Ireland. This segment will be referred to as the grey market. People in this age category have more disposable income then people in other age categories and the company's research showed that they are the most concerned about these three threatening health hazards. The Central Statistics Office estimates that by the year 2020 the number of Irish consumers over fifty-five will triple. For the second target market, there are 690,101 family households with children in the state. It is expected that this number will stay even over the next decade.

MARKETING

Pricing

Saviour Life Ltd. opted for a competitive pricing strategy. Even though the company does not have strong direct competition in Ireland, the product is available online from other sources. Saviour Life Ltd. has opted to sell the Guardian Angel at a lower price to the other direct and indirect competitors, yet still selling above cost price and therefore generating a profit.

Distribution

As mentioned previously, the target for the company is to distribute Guardian Angel throughout the fifty locations of the four main hardware stores in Ireland. The company's online service will accommodate individuals who wish to purchase the product online directly from the company. Management is also confident of securing contracts with two construction companies to purchase a minimum of 500 Guardian Angels annually. The cost of delivering the products will be incorporated into the selling price. The company can guarantee to have all orders delivered within three days. The company plans to outsource the online individual service to DHL to guarantee delivery within three days of ordering and distribute the bulk retailer's orders by means of a delivery van. The product will be stored on the company's rented premises, ready for delivery at the factory base in Dublin, and will be delivered from base to retailer.

Promotion

From the qualitative primary research conducted, it has been concluded that the company will need to demonstrate to its target audience the consequences of not having a Guardian Angel in their home as opposed to the benefits of purchasing it. In general, people tend to remember the negative aspects of things as opposed to the positive and so this should be the basis for the campaign. It has been established that people can relate to reality television. The company's research shows that there is no benefit in focusing on an informative campaign with definitions and scientific explanations as it has been found that people will not listen, as they cannot relate to such talk. In order for a marketing campaign to be successful it must have a high recall rate. After conducting in-depth interviews, it has been concluded that the company is going to opt for shock advertisement as the theme for the marketing campaign. The reason why shock advertising has been chosen is because the relevant qualitative primary research identified that this is deemed to be the most effective form of advertisement in terms of highlighting the dangers and safety.

A total of €144,000 has been allocated to the marketing budget for Year One, when the product will be launched. A further €60,000 will be spent on marketing in Year Two, and again in Year Three. The company plans to use an array of marketing channels in the campaign to advertise the Guardian Angel, including the following:

- TV advertising: Shock advertisements will be used to market the Guardian Angel and the ads will run in the evening time to appeal to both target markets. The advertisements will be broadcast on Irish television channels during peak viewing hours when the target markets will be exposed to the ads. Suitable times would include commercial breaks of the following programmes: *Six One News*, *Coronation Street*, *Eastenders*, *Fair City*, *Prime Time* and *The Late Late Show*. All of the aforementioned programmes are related to both target markets and it is felt that advertising at these times would give maximum exposure.

- Radio advertising: The company believes that an array of different radio channels needs to be discussed when advertising the product on radio in order to appeal to both target markets. A solution to this problem is a radio advertising package. A suitable package advertising a thirty second ad for twenty-three slots during prime listenership times to RTÉ Radio 1, 2FM and Lyric FM has been found to be appropriate to cover the target markets and also fits to the marketing budget requirements.
- Print advertising: Print advertisements will be included in the newspapers read by the target audiences. The company will aim to advertise in the *Irish Independent*, as it has over 180,000 daily readers and it currently holds 21.3 per cent of the 35+ market, and research from Media Live confirms that the *Irish Independent* holds the highest percentage of 35+ readers in the country. Guardian Angel will also be advertised in the *Sunday Independent*, as it has over one million readers and it currently holds 38 per cent of the 35+ market, and research from Media Live confirms that the *Sunday Independent* holds the highest percentage of 35+ readers in the country. Both the *Irish Independent* and the *Sunday Independent* offer an opportunity to advertise in their property section, which would cover advertising to homeowners buying, selling or just having a general interest in property.
- Outdoor advertising: Saviour Life Ltd. has decided to work with a promotions company called Viacom to organise all of their outdoors advertisements. The reason why the company chose Viacom is that it offers a wide range of outdoor advertising possibilities such as exploding bus t-signs, Luas opportunities, café tent cards, radius street furniture, the outbox and a range of other new ambient media opportunities.
- The Internet: A website will be created which will contain information about the Guardian Angel and the campaign and allow customers to purchase online if they wish to do so from anywhere around the globe.

OPERATIONS

Location
Saviour Life Ltd. will lease a unit in the National Digital Park on Citywest Business Campus, Co. Dublin. The location is conveniently

located adjacent to the N7, and is just two miles from the M50 orbital motorway and is a thirty minute drive from Dublin city centre. The business park is ideally located and will allow suppliers, the company's delivery van and staff easy access to and from the premises. The lease contract will include the following: two car parking spaces, general maintenance, fully fitted toilet facilities, small kitchen area with a sink, heating, air conditioning, lighting, and one desk and chair. The chosen premises conforms to all health and safety standard requirements for the workplace.

Manufacturing Process

The firm will operate from 8 a.m. to 5 p.m. with a break between 12:30 p.m. and 1:30 p.m., Monday to Friday. This results in a total of forty working hours per week. Initially two people will be employed to assemble the product in Year One. Each worker will produce a maximum of fifty units per day; approximately 400 units will be produced each week. Employees are required to assemble the final product using outsourced parts by following a number of steps under the supervision of a quality control technician. The quality control technician will train in all new employees. If sale forecasts are exceeded, overtime will be offered to the operatives. In Year Three, Saviour Life Ltd. will be earning a profit. In Year Four a percentage of profits will be retained and reinvested into research and development as the company will develop other safety devices for the home such as 'child proofing' devices. The manufacturing process for the product will be as follows:

1. The plastic base to hold the circuit board and the cover of the product will be manufactured in lots of 5,000. The circuit board will be assembled and delivered by ABC Circuits Ltd. as required to Saviour Life Ltd.
2. On delivery of all parts, 10 per cent will be inspected by the quality control technician. This is known as a batch test and ensures that there are continuous quality systems throughout the entire group of goods. The moulds will be further inspected as an operative assembles each product. All delivered parts will be stocked next to each workstation safely. The batch test will include testing the sensors and reset button. The parts will only be accepted if 95 per cent of the random batch passes the test.
3. Operatives will assemble the product in batches of ten.

4. The batches of completed products will be moved to the workstation of the quality control technician.
5. A final inspection will be carried out on all completed products. After each completed product has passed all tests it is moved to the storage section.

The equipment required to make the moulds and the electrical circuits necessary for the product is extremely expensive. For this reason the enterprise will outsource the production of all parts to a number of different suppliers. The base and cover mould to hold the finished circuit will be manufactured by Hard Plastics Ltd., while the electrical circuit board will be produced by ABC Circuits Ltd. Boxes and bubble wrap, which are necessary for the packaging of the product, will be outsourced from Bigbox Ltd. The cardboard box and bubble wrap will protect the product as it is delivered from one location to another.

Key Regulatory and Quality Issues

The organisations chosen to produce the required parts operate under all required standards. Hard Plastics has implemented a quality control system to meet the requirements of EN ISO 9002. ABC Circuits work in accordance with ISO 9001 and guarantees to place orders with manufacturers meeting certification requirements (i.e. UL, BS9000, CECC, UL 796). The "CE Marking" is the manufacturer's or importer's mark of conformity declaring compliance with all applicable directives (safety, machinery, EMC and others). The use of the "CE Marking" and "Declaration of Conformity" is now mandatory for most products and services sold in the EU. The Guardian Angel will comply with all compulsory standards and will have to obtain a CE stamp before it can go on sale.

Manufacturability and Other Operating Issues

The manufacturability was considered in designing every aspect of the product. The engineering advisor found that outsourcing was the most effective and economical way to produce the product. Through outsourcing the two essential components (the plastic housing and the electric circuit board) to two companies who specialise in these processes, the firm will benefit by not having to purchase any machinery or hire skilled workers to produce the parts. The components are designed by the two organisations in a manner that will allow for the final product to be assembled effortlessly by the operatives of Saviour Life Ltd. This means that the company can hire low-skilled workers who can be easily trained in. To ensure reliability, the product meets all safety standards (see above) and incorporates a battery failure alert. The prototype was put through vigorous tests to ensure the final product would not fail in operation. The organisations chosen to produce the two essential components have both reached satisfactory safety and quality standard regulations.

FINANCE

A minimum of €300,000 is required in order to establish Saviour Life Ltd. The company will be seeking a loan from a financial institution and will also apply for a grant from the South Dublin County Enterprise Board to raise the funds required. The €300,000 loan will be repaid to the institution over a four-year period incorporating a 5 per cent monthly interest rate. The loan will be received and spent in Year One. €100,000 will be repaid in two €50,000 installments in August and December of Year Two, and a further €50,000 repaid in both April and December of Year Three. The remainder of the loan will be repaid in two €50,000 installments in the fourth year of the business plan. The County Enterprise Board offers a number of grants for which Saviour Life Ltd. may be eligible. The company will apply for an employment grant as the firm will immediately create six new jobs and a seventh job in the beginning of the second year. The employment grant is provided to offset the costs of employing new individuals. A maximum grant of €6,350 is available for every new job created and filled. The grant is given in two installments throughout the first year of the employee's employment. The three directors of the company plan to have full 100 per cent equity. The directors will reinvest 100 per cent of the profits back into the company for the first four years.

It is projected that Saviour Life Ltd. will make a loss in the first year due to initial investment costs and the huge budget allocated for marketing and promotions covering the launch of the Guardian Angel into the market. The company also has a heavy loan to be accommodated in the first year. As the company will head into its second year, the sales are forecasted to increase and the expenditure is expected to reach a steady outflow so that the company can afford to pay back some of its loan, reducing the debt. The accounts foresee the company turning over a profit of €16,045 in Year Two and reducing their loan by €100,000. Year Three sees an ever-increasing turnover for Saviour Life Ltd. with estimated profits reaching €145,761 and again reducing the company's debt by another €100,000, leaving only a further €100,000 to be paid off in Year Four. Year One sees a gross profit margin of 11.86 per cent and similarly in Years Two and Three of 12.43 per cent and 11.28 per cent respectively. The net profit margin for Year One stands at 2.82 per cent and similarly in Years Two and Three at 3.69 per cent and 3.85 per cent respectively (cashflow, profit and loss and balance sheet projections are included in Appendix 4.1).

NOTES

1.   This case was written as a basis for class discussion rather than to illustrate either effective or ineffective handling of an administrative situation.
2.   Thomas Cooney is Director of the Institute for Minority Entrepreneurship, Dublin Institute of Technology.

Appendix 4.1 – Financial Projections: Projected Cashflow for the 12 Months Ending 31 December 2007

	Jan-07	Feb-07	Mar-07	Apr-07	May-07	Jun-07	Jul-07	Aug-07	Sep-07	Oct-07	Nov-07	Dec-07	Total
Sales			209,520	104,760	139,680	139,680	174,600	174,600	174,600	232,800	232,800	232,800	1,815,840
VAT Refund			10,933										10,933
Enterprise Ireland	19,050					19,050							38,100
Total Income	19,050	—	220,453	104,760	139,680	158,730	174,600	174,600	174,600	232,800	232,800	232,800	1,864,873
Trade Suppliers		167,305	75,287	100,383	100,383	125,479	125,479	125,479	167,305	167,305	167,305	167,305	1,489,015
Accountancy				5,000						4,000			9,000
Wages – Directors	3,750	3,750	3,750	3,750	3,750	3,750	3,750	3,750	3,750	3,750	3,750	3,750	45,000
Wages – Administration	2,585	2,585	2,585	2,585	2,585	2,585	2,585	2,585	2,585	2,585	2,585	2,585	31,020
Wages – Direct Labour	3,640	3,640	3,640	3,640	3,640	3,640	3,640	3,640	3,640	3,640	3,640	3,640	43,680
Insurance – All	1,029	1,029	1,029	1,029	1,029	1,029	1,029	1,029	1,029	1,029	1,029	1,029	12,348
Motor Expenses	950	600	600	898	600	600	600	600	1,100	600	600	600	8,348
Leasing – Van	2,854	415	415	415	415	415	415	415	415	415	415	415	7,419
Sundries & Rent	8,500	4,500	4,500	4,500	4,500	4,500	4,500	4,500	4,500	4,500	4,500	8,500	62,000
Sales Promotion & Marketing	16,000	16,000	16,000	16,000	10,000	10,000	10,000	10,000	10,000	10,000	10,000	10,000	144,000
Bank Charges			250			250			250			250	1,000
Loan Interest	1,250	1,250	1,250	1,250	1,250	1,250	1,250	1,250	1,250	1,250	1,250	1,250	15,000
VAT					46,301	43,243		55,364			64,683		209,591
Corporation Tax													
Total Expenditure	40,558	201,074	109,306	139,450	174,453	153,498	196,491	153,248	251,188	199,074	259,757	199,324	2,077,421
Opening Balance		278,492	77,418	188,565	153,875	119,102	124,334	102,443	123,795	47,208	80,934	53,976	
Balance Current Account		77,418	188,565	153,875	119,102	124,334	102,443	123,795	47,208	80,934	53,976	87,452	87,452
Directors' Loans	300,000												
Surplus/Deficit	-21,508	-201,074	111,147	-34,690	-34,773	5,232	-21,891	21,352	-76,588	33,726	-26,957	33,476	33,476
Closing Balance	278,492	77,418	188,565	153,875	119,102	124,334	102,443	123,795	47,208	80,934	53,976	87,452	87,452

Projected Cashflow for the 12 Months Ending 31 December 2008

	Jan-08	Feb-08	Mar-08	Apr-08	May-08	Jun-08	Jul-08	Aug-08	Sep-08	Oct-08	Nov-08	Dec-08	Total
Sales	232,800	232,800	232,800	232,800	256,080	256,080	256,080	279,358	279,358	291,000	291,000	291,000	3,131,156
Other Income	9,525					9,525							19,050
Total Income	242,325	232,800	232,800	232,800	256,080	265,605	256,080	279,358	279,358	291,000	291,000	291,000	3,150,206
Trade Suppliers	167,305	167,305	167,305	184,036	184,036	184,036	200,766	200,766	209,132	209,132	209,132	234,227	2,317,178
Accountancy				15,500									15,500
Wages – Directors	4,250	4,250	4,250	4,250	4,250	4,250	4,250	4,250	4,250	4,250	4,250	4,250	51,000
Wages – Administration	2,585	2,585	2,585	2,585	2,585	2,585	2,585	2,585	2,585	2,585	2,585	2,585	31,020
Wages – Direct Labour	4,853	4,853	4,853	4,853	4,853	4,853	4,853	4,853	4,853	4,853	4,853	4,853	58,236
Insurance – All	1,029	1,029	1,029	1,029	1,029	1,029	1,029	1,029	1,029	1,029	1,029	1,029	12,348
Motor Expenses	950	1,150	600	600	600	1,150	600	600	600	1,150	600	600	9,200
Leasing – Van	415	415	415	415	415	415	415	415	415	415	415	415	4,980
Sundries & Rent	6,000	6,000	6,000	6,000	6,000	6,000	6,000	6,000	6,000	6,000	6,000	12,000	78,000
Sales Promotion & Marketing	5,000	5,000	5,000	5,000	5,000	5,000	5,000	5,000	5,000	5,000	5,000	5,000	60,000
Bank Charges			270			270			270			270	1,080
Loan Interest	1,250	1,250	1,250	1,250	1,250	1,250	1,250	1,042	1,042	1,042	1,042	1,042	13,960
VAT	74,871		76,624		74,090		84,765		88,901		94,866		494,117
Corporation Tax								50,000					50,000
Loan Repayment												50,000	50,000
Total Expenditure	268,508	193,837	270,181	225,518	284,108	210,838	311,513	276,540	324,077	235,456	329,772	316,271	3,246,619
Opening Balance	87,452	61,269	100,232	62,851	70,133	42,105	96,872	41,439	44,257	-462	55,082	16,310	-8,961
Balance Current Account													
Directors' Loans													
Surplus/Deficit	-26,183	38,963	-37,381	7,282	-28,028	54,767	-55,433	2,818	-44,719	55,544	-38,772	-25,271	-25,271
Closing Balance	61,269	100,232	62,851	70,133	42,105	96,872	41,439	44,257	-462	55,082	16,310	-8,961	-8,961

Projected Cashflow for the 12 Months Ending 31 December 2009

	Jan-09	Feb-09	Mar-09	Apr-09	May-09	Jun-09	Jul-09	Aug-09	Sep-09	Oct-09	Nov-09	Dec-09	Total
Sales	325,920	325,920	337,560	337,560	337,560	337,560	337,560	337,560	337,560	349,200	349,200	349,200	4,062,360
Total Income	325,920	325,920	337,560	337,560	337,560	337,560	337,560	337,560	337,560	349,200	349,200	349,200	4,062,360
Trade Suppliers	234,227	242,593	242,593	242,593	242,593	242,593	242,593	242,593	250,958	250,958	250,958	250,958	2,936,210
Accountancy				15,500									15,500
Wages – Directors	5,000	5,000	5,000	5,000	5,000	5,000	5,000	5,000	5,000	5,000	5,000	5,000	60,000
Wages – Administration	2,585	2,585	2,585	2,585	2,585	2,585	2,585	2,585	2,585	2,585	2,585	2,585	31,020
Wages – Direct Labour	4,853	4,853	4,853	4,853	4,853	4,853	4,853	4,853	4,853	4,853	4,853	4,853	58,236
Insurance – All	1,029	1,029	1,029	1,029	1,029	1,029	1,029	1,029	1,029	1,029	1,029	1,029	12,348
Motor Expenses	950	600	600	1,150	600	600	600	1,150	600	600	600	1,150	9,200
Leasing – Van	415	415	415	415	415	415	415	415	415	415	415	415	4,980
Sundries & Rent	6,500	6,500	6,500	6,500	6,500	6,500	6,500	6,500	6,500	6,500	6,500	12,000	83,500
Sales Promotion & Marketing	5,000	5,000	5,000	5,000	5,000	5,000	5,000	5,000	5,000	5,000	5,000	5,000	60,000
Bank Charges			300			300			300			300	1,200
Loan Interest	833	833	833	625	625	625	625	625	625	625	625	417	7,916
Corporation Tax													
VAT	95,940		113,069		110,184		112,970		112,874		114,990		660,027
Loan Repayment				50,000								50,000	100,000
Total Expenditure	357,332	269,408	382,777	335,250	379,384	269,500	382,170	269,750	390,739	277,565	392,555	333,707	4,040,137
Opening Balance	-8,961	-40,373	16,139	-29,078	-26,768	-68,592	-532	-45,142	22,668	-30,511	41,124	-2,231	13,262
Balance Current Account													
Director's Loans													
Surplus/Deficit	-31,412	56,512	-45,217	2,310	-41,824	68,060	-44,610	67,810	-53,179	71,635	-43,355	15,493	15,493
Closing Balance	-40,373	16,139	-29,078	-26,768	-68,592	-532	-45,142	22,668	-30,511	41,124	-2,231	13,262	13,262

Trading Profit & Loss	2007	2008	2009
Sales	1,885,488	2,660,843	3,402,146
Other Income	38,100	19,050	—
Total Income	1,923,588	2,679,893	3,402,146
Less Cost of Sales			
Purchases	1,656,320	2,290,938	2,959,983
Direct Wages	43,680	58,236	58,236
Total Costs	1,700,000	2,349,174	3,018,219
Gross Profit	*223,588*	*330,719*	*383,927*
Less Administration Expenses			
Directors' Remuneration	45,000	51,000	60,000
Staff Salaries	31,020	31,020	31,020
Insurance	12,348	12,348	12,348
Accountancy	7,438	12,810	12,810
Bank Charges	1,000	1,080	7,916
Interest Paid	15,000	13,960	1,200
Sundries & Rent	51,240	64,463	69,008
Motor Expenses	6,899	7,603	7,603
Sales & Promotion	119,008	49,587	49,587
Depreciation	2,719	2,719	2,719
Total Expenses	291,672	246,590	254,211
Net Profit/Loss	*−68,084*	*84,129*	*129,716*

Balance Sheet	2007	2008	2009
Fixed Assets			
Motor Vehicles	10,876	8,157	5,426
Current Assets			
Trade Debtors	465,600	651,840	698,400
Bank	87,452	−8,961	13,262
Stock	—	—	—
Total Current Assets	553,052	642,879	711,662
Less Current Liabilities			
Trade Creditors	167,305	234,227	258,000
VAT	155,678	196,714	213,327
Hire Purchase	9,030	4,050	
Directors' Loan	300,000	200,000	100,000
Total Current Liabilities	632,013	634,991	571,327
	−78,961	7,888	140,335
Total Net Assets	***−68,085***	***16,045***	***145,761***
Financed By			
P&L Account	−68,084	−68,084	16,045
Profit/Loss	0	84,129	129,716
Retained Profit/Loss	***−68,085***	***16,045***	***145,761***

O'BRIENS SANDWICH BARS[1]

CHRIS O'RIORDAN, JAMES A. CUNNINGHAM AND DENIS HARRINGTON[2]

O'Briens Sandwich Bars (O'Briens) is one of Ireland's best-known brands and a leader in the gourmet coffee and sandwiches sector. Founded in the tough economic climate of the 1980s by entrepreneur Brody Sweeney, O'Briens has been developed from a small start-up into an international brand through the franchising model, and already has a global footprint in the UK, Europe and Asia. Half of O'Briens' outlets are in the UK, giving them a share of approximately 20 per cent of the UK food-focused coffee shop market. Many changes face the business, including international expansion while growing the existing business, constantly updating the brand and defending against new and bigger competitors and imitators. This is within the context of a 'changing of the guard' as a new CEO takes over the reins from the founder, creating further exciting challenges.

THE ENTREPRENEUR, THE IDEA AND THE EARLY YEARS

January 2006 marked the beginning of another chapter in the O'Briens story with the appointment of Fiacra Nagle (MD of O'Briens Ireland since 2002, having joined the organisation in 2000) as Group CEO. This move was accompanied by Brody Sweeney – founder of O'Briens – taking up the position of Executive Chairman in order to allow him time to pursue political ambitions. O'Briens was formed in 1988 when Brody opened his first store in Dublin's South Great George's Street. Brody's first foray into the world of business was at the age of 15 when he established Vico Enterprises – Tree Surgeons, a tree-cutting business. This was not as successful as Brody had hoped: one tree fell the wrong way, onto a main road, .resulting in a half-mile tailback of traffic before the fire brigade managed to remove it. Before venturing into the food retailing business, Brody ran a printing franchise (called Prontaprint) for eight years. However, this did not prove to be profitable and he sold the business in 1988. Opening up a made-to-order sandwich shop in the tough Irish economic climate of the late 1980s was considered by some observers as foolhardy. O'Briens was clearly ahead of its time, as not everyone was ready to appreciate (and pay a premium for) 'made-to-order' sandwiches. This manifested itself in the disastrous opening (and rapid closing) of the third O'Briens store in Dublin's Mary Street. From his previous two stores, Brody had learnt the importance of having a high volume of pedestrian traffic walking by the front door. The Mary Street outlet failed not because of lack of people, but rather a lack of the right people. Customers expected that they could buy two or three sandwiches for IR£1 – here were O'Briens trying to charge IR£2 for one sandwich! Needless to say, sales were not good. Within five days of opening, Brody had put the premises up for sale. It took twelve months to sell and lost money every day that passed. It was a tough lesson to learn, and almost brought the business down, but ultimately made O'Briens stronger.

It was 1994 before O'Briens secured their first franchisee. This involved Brody selling one of the existing stores – in the St. Stephen's Green Shopping Centre – to Tom Cunningham, an accountant. The store had a newsagent attached, which at the time was the more valuable part of the business. As a 'sweetener' on the deal, Brody agreed not to charge his new franchisee royalties until a further three franchises were sold. This made good business sense for all parties. From the franchisees perspective in particular, there was a period in which he was on his own in the market and, consequently, had to advertise harder for himself. However, with higher numbers of stores appearing around the area, the 'clustering' effect increased brand awareness, thus boosting trade and revenues of existing stores. O'Briens themselves estimate that when a new outlet is opened in a city or area all other stores see a 2–3 per cent increase in business. Within a short period, three more franchises were opened and Tom began paying royalties as agreed. In fact, Tom became O'Briens' first multiple franchisee when he purchased a second store and, subsequently, opened three others. Brody, himself, admits that the turning point in the business was the second sale:

> It's possible to win a trophy once or make a sale through a fluke or through good salesmanship. Being able to do so more than once takes the strength and depth that only a great team has (Sweeney, 2005).

Brody created the O'Briens name as he felt he needed a catchy title, something that would distinguish his company, but that would also bring out the 'Irishness' of the business. He found, from the phonebook, that O'Brien was one of the most popular names in Ireland and he settled on this. Indeed, the 'Irishness' of the business has come more to the fore in recent years as O'Briens has expanded internationally – the quality association appeals to customers, many of whom have never even been to Ireland. Today, O'Briens have found that the 'Irish' angle is of much less significance in Ireland and the UK, to the point that they have renamed themselves "O'Briens Sandwich Bars" in these countries.

THE PRODUCT

There are four elements to the O'Briens brand, three of which are based around the store itself:

The Food

Customers can buy pre-prepared sandwiches in an O'Briens' outlet, but the focus of each store is on made-to-order sandwiches. Customers can choose from their trademarked food such as Wrappo™, Toostie™, juices and gourmet coffee from Vietnam, which is grown on farms that the company supports through its sponsorship of the Christina Noble Children's Foundation. O'Briens market guilt-free food by emphasising to customers that they can watch the calories and still have delicious food (see Exhibit 5.1).

To maintain brand consistency the support office controls the choice of suppliers from which franchisees can purchase. This ensures that only quality ingredients are used across the stores and that all products are fully traceable, as Fiacra explains:

> We work with nominated suppliers, so any franchisee is obliged to buy only from these and they meet our criteria, so that keeps

Exhibit 5.1
Guilt Free Foods: Bread

		Kcal/O'Briens Portion	G fat/portion
Bread, White Thin Slices	2 Slices	220 kcal	1.6 gms
Bread, Brown, Thin Slices	2 Slices	230 kcal	1.4 gms
Tortilla Wrap	1 Wrap	183 kcal	0.7 gms
Classic Bagel	1 Bagel	231 kcal	1.4 gms

Source: http://www.obriens.ie/MAIN/Food/guiltfree/default.asp

us comfortable that the traceability is there and the quality and consistency ... we have to be able to offer the same product across all of our stores.

This can cause occasional conflict with franchisees, who may wish to deal with a local supplier who is selling at a discount, but O'Briens remain firm on this, as Fiacra points out:

We can't guarantee that and it also puts more risk on the business.

However, where possible, O'Briens will try to use Irish produce in their stores, but for international outlets, this is clearly more challenging and requires some compromise. Given that the 18–35 age market remains key to O'Briens' success, they use a number of organic products, as Fiacra explains:

We use organic milk, because we have it at the right price point and its not going to change the price of our coffee.

However, it is not practical to go completely organic, as some products would result in a price that would ultimately be difficult to justify.

The Shop
In the early years, O'Briens established small outlets in order to achieve critical mass – their Grafton Street store in Dublin is approximately

300 square feet. However, today the focus is on size as, primarily, the management team are interested in properties of 1,200–1,300 square feet in busy lunchtime areas to accommodate their Mark 3 stores. This increased space allows a greater offering – including juice bars – and more seating to accommodate higher traffic. However, the shops maintain their singular corporate identity with the same green colour scheme, standard menus (with some cultural adaptation), Irish background music and modern equipment. This consistency is important, as an O'Briens in Singapore or Spain is as equally identifiable as a store in Cork or Glasgow. The actual location of the shop is critical and O'Briens put a considerable amount of effort into sourcing prime properties. Airports, busy pedestrian areas near to offices and shopping centres are optimal locations as the success of an outlet is, in part, dependent on having considerable numbers of people walking (not driving) by. The company takes an active role in the site search, through their property team, and will vet all locations. O'Briens take out the actual lease of the property for two important reasons:

(a) Leasers are happier to deal with an established, recognised and financially healthy business than with a franchisee who is going into business for the first time and

(b) If there is any breakdown in the relationship between O'Briens and the franchisee, O'Briens hold the lease and can sub-let to a new business.

Customer Service

Training and evaluation of store staff is critical to maintain high-quality standards, and O'Briens focus strongly on this. At the outset, all new franchise owners receive four weeks of training. Two weeks are spent in O'Briens' support office in a classroom setting, with two further weeks being spent in a dedicated training store. It is preferred that franchisees work full-time in their stores as this ensures that they are on the ground, dealing with issues when they happen rather than letting problems build. By being trained in customer service themselves, franchisees can ensure that their staff know what is expected of them. O'Briens handle the on-site training of all staff once they have been hired and this is an ongoing process for all. In 2004, all franchisees were retrained at a one-day course. The company is very conscious that the franchise is more than just a name, it is a 'package' with multiple elements and wide-ranging support, and this is one of its main selling points, as Rory Smyth, the Group's International Manager notes:

> We are a true, full-service franchise, as opposed to just a licence.

To ensure that training is embedded from the outset and that standards are being maintained, O'Briens carry out regular service evaluations through the use of 'mystery customers' and act on the results of these. Brody is a firm believer in 'walking the walk' and, when in franchisees' stores, if he sees a table or floor that isn't clean, he cleans it up himself:

> This sends a message to the storeowner that I am prepared to put in the work on the ground myself – quite literally! (Sweeney, 2005)

Furthermore, as a means of emphasising the importance of the customer, all O'Briens support staff – regardless of their role – must spend one day every six months working behind the counter at an outlet. This ensures that everyone knows who exactly they are really working for. As Brody himself commented in his recent book:

> I still get a great sense of excitement and achievement from see-ing a full car park outside an O'Briens store or standing behind a till, slightly incredulous that people are happy to hand over their hard-earned cash for the privilege of eating and drinking in one of our stores (Sweeney, 2005).

Catering and Retail Offer

O'Briens recognise that basing all of their sales around physical outlets limits their scope. The outside catering arm serves two important purposes – as a further revenue stream and as a means of advertising the product. This has been extended further with O'Briens selling sandwich fillings, coleslaw and salads through shops and supermarkets. The distribution of these products is handled through Kerry Fresh, a division of Kerry Foods plc, a major international food ingredients producer. By selling the ingre-dients via retail outlets, O'Briens are targeting customers who might not otherwise be buying an O'Briens sandwich, namely those who like to make a packed lunch or who are too far from an outlet to make it feasible to visit. This has generated adverse reaction from some franchisees, but Fiacra Nagle does not feel there is any justification, and explains:

> They think they might lose customers because of this, but I think it is more of an emotional response rather than a firm view. Our business and like-for-like sales are growing, and this is just enhancing our brand equity. If you are sitting in an office and you decide that you are going to go and buy a roll and coleslaw or sandwich mix and chicken, that decision has already been made, you're going to go to the supermarket anyway. We want to pick up that market.

This exercise has proved successful to date and the company is expanding on it in the future, possibly by developing a retail coffee pack. The key, however, is to ensure that sales are not just cannibalising the existing business.

MARKET TRENDS AND COMPETITION

By the beginning of 2006 O'Briens had over 280 stores worldwide, with approximately 50 per cent of these in the UK. The UK operation is managed through a support office in London. O'Briens are seeking to expand into new international territories using the franchise model of expansion, through a development agent or master franchiser. Their priority countries include all EU counties, Japan, USA and Canada. The goal is to have 1,000 stores operating by 2008. The UK market is very competitive; O'Briens (UK) lost £718,000 in 2003 and owed its Irish parent € 3.14 million.

In 2005, according to the British Sandwich Association (http://www.sandwichesonline.org.uk/sandwich_soapbox/viewtopic.php?t=43), the UK sandwich market was estimated to be worth £3.5 billion, which was over three times as much as was spent on pizzas. Approximately 1.8 billion sandwiches are sold commercially, while considerably more are made at home. More men than women buy commercially made sandwiches, while over 44 per cent of all sandwich buyers are in the 24-to-44 age bracket. Cafés and sandwich bars account for just under 16 per cent of sandwiches purchased, 6 per cent less than supermarkets, while half of all workers in the UK typically purchase food during the working day to consume at work for lunch or as a snack. Estimates of market growth in the purchase of food and drink for consumption at work continues to rise at an annual rate of 0.06 per cent per annum, which is faster than the increase in the total population of

0.04 per cent per annum. UK statistics for 2004 show that, "The average spend per worker for snacks to eat during the working day is over 50% more than the equivalent spend on lunch foods. This anomaly reflects the importance of snacking at the workplace and charts the growing importance of snack products and convenient snack style meals" (Mintel, 2005).

According to Datamonitor (2005c) the UK fast food market grew by 4.1 per cent in 2004 (CAGR 2000–2004: 3.3 per cent) and was valued at $4.9 billion. Quick service restaurants held nearly 60 per cent of the market share, whereas takeaways only accounted for 12.1 per cent. In European terms, the UK market accounts for over 20 per cent of Europe's fast food market value. The European fast food market growth was more moderate. In 2005 the market grew by 3 per cent and was valued at $21.8 billion, with forecasts of it being valued at $25.4 billion by 2009. In 2004 quick service restaurants accounted for 54.5 per cent of European market value (see Exhibit 5.2).

There has been a gradual decline in sandwich consumption in the US even though it still is the number one food prepared at home, with 36 per cent

Exhibit 5.2
UK and European Fast Food Market Statistics

	UK	European
Market Value $ Billion		
2003	4.7	21.2
2004	4.9	21.8
Market Volume: Transactions Billion		
2003	1.7	10.6
2004	1.748	10.7
Market Segmentation:		
Quick Service Restaurants	59.6 %	54.5 %
Leisure Locations	27.6 %	26.7 %
Takeaways	12.1 %	16 %
Mobile & Street Vendor	0.6 %	2.8 %

Source: Adapted from Datamonitor 'Reports of the Fast Food Industry in Europe and the UK', August 2005.

of home-prepared lunch meals including this menu item. In 1985, 40 per cent of all lunches included a sandwich.

Coffee dominated the European hot drinks market in 2004, accounting for 70.1 per cent of the total value, with supermarkets being the main distribution channel. In global terms, the European hot drinks market is the largest in the world, accounting for 47.8 per cent. In 2004, the UK tea market accounted for 56.2 per cent of its value and the overall market volume shrank by 0.5 per cent in 2005. Overall the compounded annual growth rate of the market volume in the period 2001–2005 was 0.3 per cent (see Exhibit 5.3).

US consumers are willing to pay up to $5 for gourmet coffee, while the rate of consumption in 2005 was lower than it was in 2000 and coffee consumption fell below hot tea for the first time in 2004. In Ireland, the

Exhibit 5.3
UK and European Hot Drink Market Statistics

	UK	European
Market Value $ Billion		
2003	4.27	25.9
2004	4.30	26.3
2005 (estimate)	4.30	26.6
Market Volume: Transactions kgs Million		
2003	254.3	2,730.1
2004	254.3	2,776.9
2005 (estimate)	252.9	2,824.7
Market Segmentation % Share by Value, 2005		
Coffee	26.4 %	70.1 %
Tea	56.2 %	21.5 %
Other Hot Drinks	17.3 %	8.4 %

Source: Adapted from Datamonitor 'Reports of the Hot Drinks Industry in Europe and the UK', December 2005.

sandwich and takeaway coffee sector is estimated to be worth €250 million, with takeaway sandwiches accounting for 14 per cent of all eating out.

Health concerns surrounding the consumption of food from fast food outlets has become a real concern for governments, health insurers, food ingredients manufacturers and fast food outlets. The dramatic rise in obesity in the US is mirrored in Europe. In Ireland it is estimated that one in eight adults and one in twenty children are obese, while it is believed that 20 per cent of European children are overweight. These concerns have filtered into the marketplace. McDonald's, a franchise competitor of O'Briens, now offers 'healthy options' and provides consumers with information about calorie counts for their food. Such is the potential growth in obesity that some national governments are considering introducing a fat tax on food.

One of O'Briens' main competitors in Ireland (for food and drink) is Insomnia. Founded in 1998, the company has twenty-three outlets (twenty in Dublin) with plans to reach fifty outlets in 2007. Insomnia's turnover in 2005 hit €10 million, double that of 2004. Media speculation in 2004 surrounded Insomnia as they are seen as a suitable acquisition vehicle for Starbucks expansion in the Irish market. Starbucks entered the Irish coffee and snacks market in 2005, opening four stores in Dublin. Neither Insomnia nor Starbucks use the franchising model, establishing only wholly owned stores. In international markets, Prêt à Manger, Starbucks, Caffé Nero, Costa Coffee, Subway and Coffee Republic compete in dealing premium food and coffee. Reflecting on these changes, Fiacra Nagle comments:

> When we started off, there weren't a huge amount of competitors and we were doing sandwiches, coffee and soup as the main cornerstones of the business. Now there are expanded food concessions in convenience stores and new coffee outlets. It is a crowded marketplace here and abroad, as the market changes to suit modern lifestyle (O'Brien-Lynch, 2006).

O'BRIENS' UNIQUENESS, MARKETING AND CORPORATE SOCIAL RESPONSIBILITY (CSR): PROTECTING AGAINST IMITATORS

According to O'Briens, "Our success has been based on simplicity".

Ultimately, what O'Briens do is sell high-quality sandwiches, gourmet coffee and complementary extras such as wraps, desserts and juices; this, in itself, is simple. But as Rory Smyth says:

> How we do it, possibly, is how we are different and better as
> opposed to anything else ... we deliver an experience that is better
> than anyone else: the quality of the food, the ambience, the staff,
> the training. We go bigger into the business.

New Product Development

O'Briens have a new product development team constantly seeking new
ways of updating the product offering, as Fiacra recognises:

> There is a risk that people will copy us and our work ...
> Convenience stores are now offering made-to-order sandwiches;
> every pub in the country seems to have a cappuccino machine. These
> are not as unique to O'Briens as they were in the early days.

Being different means trying new ideas and a willingness to experiment
and, for O'Briens, this means attending international food exhibitions and
bringing home products that are a bit different. Not all of these experi-
ments are successful – a test on using Atkins-friendly bread in making
sandwiches was not popular with customers, since, as Rory highlights:

> [I]f you're on the Atkins diet, you don't eat sandwiches.

Successful products will be those that fit the brand portfolio, that are
feasible, that are supported by the franchisees and that are profitable. O'Briens are not interested in simply copying what everyone else is
doing and, consequently, do not sell paninis. Instead, they have developed and branded their own product called the 'Shambo™'. As Fiacra
explains:

> We liked the idea of branding a sandwich; by giving it a name that
> we could hang our hat on and use it in our marketing ... we wanted
> to be different, with an O'Briens' twist to it.

Marketing

Strengthening the brand, through marketing and standardisation of operations, is central to O'Briens' expansion. The company is renowned for its
use of PR and sees great benefits in this. O'Briens try to send out at least

one press release a month to a group of press people, which, according to Fiacra, has led to the company establishing itself:

> [A]s the reference point for the sandwich and coffee market in Ireland, so people talk to us and we get coverage.

O'Briens believe that the use of PR, particularly in the early days, helped to make the company appear bigger and more successful than it was – a knock-on benefit of this was making the franchise even more attractive, as Sweeney (2005) notes:

> [W]e talked about the number of coffee beans we used each year, which sounded very impressive until you translated that into actual cups of coffee and then into cash – by which time it wasn't very interesting at all.

The company limit their central marketing spend to 3 per cent of what they collect weekly from franchisees. This allows for an annual spend, in Ireland, of less than €1 million, considerably less than what many advertisers pitching to O'Briens think is available. The company engage in some limited, but focused, media marketing. In 2004 the company launched a series of TV ads for the first time to promote their "guilt free foods". In recognition of their target audience, the ads were humorous, in the style of a fly-on-the wall documentary, and based in an office around an embarrassing incident. The ad finishes with the line "Whatever else you feel guilty about, you needn't feel as guilty about lunch". In 2005, O'Briens sponsored the lunchtime slot on Today FM, Ireland's largest independent national radio station (listenership of 135,000). The company have also employed what they refer to as 'guerrilla marketing'. Some years ago, to get the company noticed, Brody and his brother would hang banners off bridges and flyovers over busy Dublin roads with the company's name on them. Dublin Corporation, not surprisingly, removed these and confiscated them but the only loss was the cost of the banner. After a while, Brody realised that:

> [M]ost of the Corporation guys didn't work weekends or bank holidays, which meant that at times of heavy traffic movements, our banners went undisturbed.
>
> We had a long period when we would put the banners up on a Friday evening and remove them again on a Sunday evening. In

the intervening period, literally tens of thousands of people were exposed to our logo, at almost no cost. All of this helped fill our stores and popularise our brand (Sweeney, 2005).

Most of the actual marketing is based around the stores. Franchisees are aware that the central marketing is the minimum that is required from their perspective. For their 3 per cent, they receive a regular delivery of promotional material – posters, flyers – but are expected to do their own local marketing as well. O'Briens have established that their core market is within a 500-yard radius of the outlet and, consequently, promotions need to be targeted in this area. This is particularly important when a new store is being opened, where awareness is most critical, as Sweeney (2005) notes:

From handing out balloons outside the store on a Saturday, to walking around with free samples, to doing direct-mail shots to businesses that were close to us, we hit our target market in a regular and persistent way, and conveniently in ways that were cheaper, relatively, than other methods.

Each new store opening also generates a press release, with some biographical information about the franchisee included to increase their profile. Occasionally, larger events are built around outlets and these generate their own media attention (see Exhibit 5.4).

Marketing for, and in, international outlets presents additional challenges. While Ireland and the UK have embraced the 'purchased' sandwich culture (with average lunch times of 35–40 minutes), this is not as common elsewhere. In particular, this has proven a difficulty in breaking into continental Europe. O'Briens' failure to crack the market in Denmark (even though the team was led by a former MD of McDonald's in Scandinavia) was essentially down to two factors. Firstly, the 'clustering' that has proven successful in Ireland did not happen – the initial two stores were over four hours travel time apart, reducing their impact and making their management more challenging. Secondly, O'Briens discovered that – like a number of other countries nearby – the Danes, at that point, were still predominantly a 'lunch box nation':

They didn't spend €5 or €6 on lunch; instead they brought a packed lunch (Rory Smyth).

Exhibit 5.4
Examples of Increasing Brand Profile

- The Scottish franchise team, in October 2005, beat the record for the World's Tallest Sandwich (at 45 feet) that had previously been set by their colleagues in Cork two years earlier. The event helped to raise funds for the Christina Noble Children's Foundation.
- O'Briens have held an annual Photographer of the Year competition for the last seven years: the six winning photographs each year (based on a theme) are turned into postcards that are displayed in all O'Briens outlets worldwide.
- O'Briens Annual Coffee Campaign in Singapore was launched, in February 2005, by 'Big Rory', a world-renowned stilt walker who was the first person to ever ski on stilts!

Source: O'Briens website (http://www.obriens.ie)

This was an important discovery for the company and they learned from the error for future destinations. Initially, the same situation was arising in the Netherlands, but

> It's changing and, in the year now that they have been open, our Dutch franchisee is noticing more and more people coming in. At the start, he was wondering where everyone was. It seems to be a cultural thing (Rory Smyth).

For marketing purposes, O'Briens was traditionally a business that focussed mainly on the 18–35 year olds, as this has been their target market (mainly female, white-collar/professional, good disposable income, health conscious). However, while a profitable group, this is also a fickle group and, with so much choice available to consumers, O'Briens are aware of the need to insulate themselves against market shifts. Attracting children to the store is a wise tactic, because children bring adults, as Rory notes:

> In the past they weren't our core business but now we know we need to get them in as they bring parents.

This has involved making the menus 'fun' and attractive to children, while remaining healthy (being attractive to the accompanying adult). Moreover, the newer stores are designed in a more family-friendly layout, with juice bars and smoothies to bring in the younger customer. Traditionally, this was one of McDonald's key markets and how they will respond in the coming years will be interesting.

Corporate Social Responsibility (CSR)

O'Briens are major advocates of the CSR concept on many levels. At store level, franchisees are encouraged to play an active role in the communities they work and live in. This can involve such activities as sponsoring local teams, providing free sandwiches to the local active retirement group and allowing community organisations to use the shop in the evenings for meetings. These are relatively inexpensive contributions, but have a considerable impact, as Fiacra explains:

> [I]f people in an area see that our franchisees are working as part of the community, they will generally think better of them as a business, and they will be more inclined to use them.

On a corporate level, the company acts in a similar manner but on a larger scale. O'Briens is the premier worldwide sponsor of the Christina Noble Children's Foundation (http://www.cncf.org/). The foundation, headed by Christina Noble, was founded in 1989 to help children in need in Vietnam and Mongolia with education, accommodation, care and job opportunities. O'Briens have pledged to build sixteen homes annually in these countries, bring young people to Ireland and train them in restaurant management, fund shelters and schools as well as the running of the residential Sunshine Ger Village in Mongolia where fifty children are cared for by seventeen full-time staff. To raise some of the funding required O'Briens hold an annual sponsored cycle in which the directors, franchisees, staff, suppliers and friends of O'Briens participate.

In 2003 Ireland hosted the Special Olympics and O'Briens pledged €1.27m to the event – the first time the event had been held outside of the US and the largest worldwide sporting event that year. O'Briens were one of the main sponsors of the event, arising out of a documentary that Brody saw about the 1999 Games. With two of his godsons having learning disabilities, he felt a need to contribute. The company held many events to raise the required cash, such as a sponsored cycle, a white-tie ball, a golf classic (raising €250,000), an art auction and a concert, as well as having moneyboxes in all stores. During the games O'Briens looked after the feeding of all athletes and all of those involved in the events. This was a major logistical task, as not only were the participants widely dispersed, but also culture and religion had to be considered in preparing the meals for some of the international teams. Overall, the games instilled an even greater sense of team spirit within the company and between the company and its associates. They received very valuable PR from being involved, but see this as a fringe benefit and not the reason for participating in the first place, as Sweeney (2005) states:

> While your staff and customers will applaud you for making the right decision, they will see through a cynical effort which is deemed to be exploitative or inappropriate. If you really aren't passionate about helping others in some way, maybe it would be better not to bother.

INTERNATIONALISATION: THE FRANCHISE MODEL

A major factor in O'Briens' success has been its attraction as a franchise opportunity. The internationalisation of O'Briens, while part of Brody's plan for the business, came about quite fortuitously. In 1997 a British accountant by the name of Hugh Hoyes-Cock contacted Brody expressing an interest in setting up an O'Briens in Singapore, where he was based. Hugh had heard about Brody's business from his son, Alex, who was studying in Dublin and regularly lunched at O'Briens. Alex spoke very highly of the outlet and Hugh decided to see it for himself. Hugh became the master franchiser for Asia and started the ball rolling on O'Briens' international adventure. This approach has been replicated in other regions where O'Briens have been established. Ideally, O'Briens seek to deal with a single master franchiser in a country or area who has intimate local knowledge and contacts. Because of the considerable distance and time differences involved, having someone trustworthy and ambitious on the ground is essential. The master franchiser is responsible for growing and expanding the business in their region – they negotiate franchise agreements with single operators (within terms defined by O'Briens' support office) and maintain these agreements. O'Briens are not always a party to such agreements – they exercise their control via an agreement with the master franchiser. However, the company is conscious that this break in the chain of control can be dangerous. As a result, they ensure that local legal experts vet all contracts entered into – this is particularly important in countries where the legal systems are different to those in Ireland and the UK. In recent years, the company has seen the benefit of having "watertight" agreements, as a very small number of franchisees have attempted to pull out of their contracts and run the stores themselves. O'Briens deal with such breaches strongly and swiftly as they are very careful to be seen not just to have solid contracts, but also to be seen enforcing them, sending an important message.

At the core of the concept is O'Briens' Operational Manual. This is, essentially, the "rules of the game" for franchisees, a knowledge repository of how to run the business. The manual puts a structure around something that is essentially entrepreneurial and, as the business grew, the importance of this became even more noticeable:

> Initially, we might have been a little too enthusiastic and let people away with too much. In recent years, because I've been doing the deals with people, I've been able to put the structures in place that we need (Rory Smyth).

When a franchisee is unsure of what to do in a particular situation, their first point of reference is the manual. This can also avoid conflicts arising later – the support office has, in writing, what is expected and how matters should be handled. The company also has a Master Franchiser's Operational Manual in place to guide master franchisers in other territories. Because of the distances involved, this is essential and is a detailed document, reinforcing O'Briens' concept of consistency worldwide, as Sweeney (2005) states:

> It tells them how to conduct their franchisee interviews, how to do their property searches and so on. That is their bible.

O'Briens are conscious of not trying to "micro-manage" because they are aware that the type of franchisees that they attract want to be involved because they like the freedom of running a business. The support office sees its role, for established international franchises, as being to get them to where their counterparts in Ireland and the UK are – multiple outlets. This is a challenge, but they perceive that the hard work is already done as the brand has been embedded:

> Our expertise should really now be in how do we help them to open 30 or 40 stores (Sweeney, 2005).

O'Briens market the quality of supplier partners, the ability to rent prime retail sites, store track records, consistency of their product along with a strong brand as unique aspects of their franchise offering. O'Briens are keen to keep the cost of setting up an outlet at a level that is affordable, but that is expensive enough so that only those committed to the concept can handle it. As franchises go, the O'Briens model is competitively priced. In Ireland, franchisees can expect to have an initial capital outlay in the range of €100,000 to €150,000, depending on the size of the store. In the UK, an O'Briens outlet will require franchisee investment of approximately £150,000 compared to Costa Coffee's £250,000 liquid assets and the ability to raise a further £500,000 without having to borrow against the initial stores opened. O'Briens also notice that in periods during which there have been redundancies, demand for franchise opportunities can increase.

INTERNATIONAL EXPANSION: SUCCESSES AND FAILURES

The success of rolling out the franchise model internationally has been mixed. Entering the Spanish market had some initial difficulties. O'Briens' first store was set up in Marbella, an ideal location because of the volumes of Irish and UK tourists in the summer and expatriates all year round. The local trade has also flourished and the franchisee has noticed that the traditional custom of tapas and long lunches is changing: people want quick and convenient food. However, the second store in Fuengirola – in a shopping centre – started quite slowly. The franchisee observed that, while traffic was high, customers were coming in and leaving again. The root of the problem was that they did not know what they were supposed to do:

> We have a 'made-to-order' concept and they are looking at the menus, confused as to what they should do next. Rather than ask, we have found that many will just leave (Rory Smyth).

To overcome this problem, the company launched a promotional campaign whereby leaflets (in Spanish) are given to customers when they arrive outlining how to order, from selecting the bread type and fillings to what drink they would like. This has proven successful and was a case of adapting the O'Briens concept to local culture.

While such adaptation is important, it is critical that it does not stretch too far. Consistency of style and offering is important across O'Briens outlets, and too much change can confuse what the brand is about. An example of this arose in the Taiwanese franchise. O'Briens noticed that the franchisees' sales were falling quite badly and received a visit from Hugh, the master franchiser for the region. He discovered that the store was using waiters! Customers came into the restaurant, waited to be seated and ordered from the table rather than at the counter. This had two notable impacts: firstly, the customers did not get an opportunity to see the ingredients being nicely presented and reduced the opportunity of an "impulse buy" of a smoothie or a dessert, and secondly, if all the tables were busy, customers simply left rather than queuing at the counter. The company took a hard line on this and the franchisee agreed to drop the table service. Sales began to increase again, as had been predicted. O'Briens see this as part of their role: educating customers and franchisees in the best way of doing business.

One of O'Briens' biggest disappointments in their 18-year existence has been their failure in the United States; established only a few short years earlier, O'Briens' US venture – "Brody's Sandwich Bars" – closed in 2004. According to O'Briens' financial statements, the US operation had lost $400,000 in the year ending 31 December 2003 and owed €747,000 to the Irish business. The US operation could not use the "O'Briens" trade name because this was already in use by another business, however, the company do not feel that this hampered the establishment of the brand or creating recognition because no one in the US knew of the Irish company anyway. It did, however, present some operational inconveniences:

> For most of our businesses abroad, we can simply transfer a lot of the Irish materials over. But, in the US, it didn't make sense to print 'Brody's Coffee Cups' because the run wasn't enough. We were missing out on a lot of things there associated with the brand because it didn't make sense to print for just one store (Rory Smyth).

The company opened their first store in Chicago, having been approached by an interested franchisee. O'Briens had to guarantee the debts of their US company as franchise legislation in the US is very much in favour of protecting the franchisee. The store did not perform well and, with the legal position acting against them, O'Briens recruited the franchisee as an employed development agent of the company. A second store was opened and the company sold a further franchise; again, both performed very poorly. The company identified the problem as two-fold. Firstly, the development agent was not working out and secondly, the poor performance of existing stores meant that interest in further franchises was non-existent. O'Briens made the decision to withdraw from the market.

THE FUTURE

As Fiacra Nagle prepares for his first board meeting as group CEO, he knows that the future for O'Briens holds many interesting challenges. Developing a global footprint for the brand and protecting against imitators are key issues. O'Briens are a major player in the Irish and UK convenience food market and are a sought-after franchising opportunity. The immediate goal is to conquer the UK and gain a critical mass in the market akin to their position in Ireland so that they can be profitable and achieve easier growth. Establishing a greater presence in continental Europe is also important, but selecting the right countries, entry strategies and cross-cultural issues cause added complexity. While returning to the US is not entirely ruled out, it may be more of a medium-term target. However, the US market is showing a recovery and there would now appear to be an opportunity for O'Briens to establish themselves as the number two to Starbucks. New ideas are not easy to come by, but franchisees demand these, as they need to see growth in their own stores. Their successes advertise the brand as much as anything else. Not only that, but the threat of new competitors remains strong in the Irish market; the dominance of one or two players must be interesting some of the major UK chains. How does O'Briens defend against such a scenario? Brody's appointment as Executive Chairman ensures continuity of the O'Briens culture and ethos, but Fiacra knows that constantly refining O'Briens' uniqueness and defining their "guilt-free food" will be the focus of his tenure as group CEO. As he points out:

> I don't see myself ever having the same profile as Brody. I'm a different style of operator. He will always be associated with the brand and I hope I will be associated with it as well but in a different way (O'Brien-Lynch, 2006).

Only time will tell.

Acknowledgements

This case was made possible by the cooperation of the staff and management of O'Briens Irish Sandwich Bars Limited. A special note of thanks to Fiacra Nagle, Rory Smyth and Elaine Mellon for their very generous assistance in bringing this case to fruition.

References

Datamonitor (2005a) 'Hot Drinks in the United Kingdom: Industry Profile', London: December.

Datamonitor (2005b) 'Hot Drinks in Europe: Industry Profile', London: December.

Datamonitor (2005c) 'Fast Food in the United Kingdom: Industry Profile', London: August.

Datamonitor (2005d) 'Fast Food in Europe: Industry Profile', London: August.

Kenny, I. (2005) *Achievers – Visionary Irish Leaders Who Achieved Their Dreams*, Dublin: Oak Tree Press.

Mintel (2005) 'Eating at Work – UK – December 2005', Mintel Group.

O'Brien-Lynch, R. (2006) 'Nagle has appetite for O'Briens Expansion Plan', *Irish Times*, 13 January 2006.

Sweeney, Brody (2005) *Making Bread – The Real Way to Start Up and Stay Up in Business*, Dublin: Liberties Press.

Interviews

Nagle, Fiacra (2005): Group CEO of O'Briens Irish Sandwich Bars, interview conducted 11 November 2005.

Smyth, Rory (2005): International Manager of O'Briens Irish Sandwich Bars, interview conducted 11 November 2005.

NOTES

1. This case was written as a basis for class discussion rather than to illustrate either effective or ineffective handling of an administrative situation.

2. Mr Chris O'Riordan is a lecturer in Accounting at Waterford Institute of Technology. Dr Denis Harrington is Head of Graduate Business also at Waterford Institute of Technology. Dr James A. Cunningham is the Executive MBA Programme Director and lectures in strategy and entrepreneurship at the J.E. Cairnes Graduate School of Business & Public Policy, NUI, Galway.

THE BUTLER'S PANTRY[1]

GERALDINE LAVIN[2]

The Butler's Pantry has firmly established itself as a brand leader in producing and retailing high-quality 'food to go', trading on their promise to the customer of "natural ingredients, delicious recipes, hand prepared – from our kitchen to yours." The Butler's Pantry was established in 1987 by Eileen Bergin. Eileen had long been convinced that a niche existed in the ready meals market for fresh, high-quality chilled meals. She had seen the idea work in America and Canada and, as no one was doing it in Ireland at the time, Eileen felt that the opportunity was there to be exploited.

The company has a strong image in its marketplace and would be perceived to be at the top of its market segment. It has received numerous awards reflecting its strong market position, including the Bridgestone Award every year since 1995, the small business award at the Irish Food and Drink Industry Awards in 2003 and 2004, and the Small Firms Association National Retailer of the Year Award at the National Small Business Awards in 2005.

The rapid growth of the business is testament to Eileen's foresight – from sales on the first day of twelve meals, some breads and a few cookies in one shop, the business has now grown to selling nearly 2,000 meals a day, along with a variety of breads and a vast array of desserts, in six shops as well as having a growing wholesale business. (See Appendix 6.1 for details of The Butler's Pantry's Business Milestones.)

Despite experiencing year-on-year growth since its establishment in 1987, The Butler's Pantry is facing an increasingly competitive marketplace. The management team have identified a number of possibilities for expansion and business development, namely expanding the wholesale market, increasing the number of shops and expanding their product ranges and services. However, should they focus on one area or try a number of approaches? Also, can they grow the business in the face of strengthening competition while still maintaining the integrity of the brand they have worked so hard to build?

THE HIGH-QUALITY CHILLED FOOD MARKET

The ready meals market comprises of three main segments:

1. Frozen foods (the largest sub-segment), such as frozen vegetables and pizza.
2. Ambient foods, including dried and canned products, such as dried pulses, dried fruits and tinned vegetables.
3. Chilled foods, usually pre-made meals, which is the sub-segment seen as the most dynamic and the one experiencing the greatest growth.

The chilled foods market is experiencing rapid growth and is constantly changing as customers' needs develop. Research by the Ashtown Food Research Centre[3] (Henchion, 2000) highlights the consumer trends driving the overall demand for ready meals, including:

- Changing demographics and smaller household size.
- More women working.
- Loss of cooking skills.
- Income growth.
- Breakdown of the family meal due to more individual lifestyles.
- Time pressures for meal preparation (in many homes, the main meal of the day is prepared in less than 30 minutes as opposed to about 2.5 hours during the 1930s).

The chilled food market is a sophisticated one, comprised mainly of consumers from the A and B demographics. Consumers of The Butler's Pantry product are an educated market with money to spend. They are influenced a lot by travel out of Ireland, which is reflected in the food choices they request in The Butler's Pantry shops. The market is growing primarily because of lifestyle; consumers are time-poor and cash-rich with discerning palates. Generally, both partners in a household are working, increasing the need for quick, quality food. These consumers tend to be very conscious about what they are eating and are concerned with food traceability – an ideal consumer group for The Butler's Pantry and its high-quality product. The aforementioned research by the Ashtown Food Research Centre (Henchion, 2000) indicates that the Irish market for ready meals is currently small but experiencing rapid growth. Although up-to-date market size figures are not available for the Irish market, it is estimated that per capita consumption of ready meals in Ireland is about one-third of that in the UK, with the implication being that there is still significant room for growth. Sales growth in Irish chilled foods received a boost from an unexpected source in 2004. The ban on smoking in the workplace, which obviously includes food outlets, has led to a change in dining habits, as more people decided to dine and entertain at home. Paolo Tullio, the renowned restaurant reviewer and wine correspondent for the *Irish Independent*, commented that:

> Gourmet meals like The Butler's Pantry are picking up disaffected smokers as new customers as they stay at home to puff on the killer weed (www.tasteofireland.com/review.rvt/1113.html).

The research by the Ashtown Food Research Centre (Henchion, 2000) further reveals that chilled food is perceived by customers to be fresher and healthier than frozen or ambient food. Price is generally not an issue for customers, as they expect to pay more for chilled food, however quality and product range are key issues for customers. This research is reinforced by a recent Mintel report (2004) on chilled meals in the UK, which reports that, while convenience is key to the success of chilled ready meals, quality distinguishes the category from competitive products. This research also highlights that consumers perceive the meals are fresh and reasonably healthy, tapping into the growing awareness of healthy eating.

In recent years, strong competition has come into the market and it is very intense. In the chilled ready meals market, Marks & Spencer dominate, carrying up to 140 different chilled meal lines. There has also been an expansion in the number of chilled meals carried by the other major supermarkets, indicating the attractiveness of the market. As well as these large-scale competitors, other indigenous competitors are coming into the market, such as Cully and Sully, a Cork-based company that prepares, markets and distributes high-quality ready meals to supermarkets and pubs in Ireland, some featuring recipes from the world-renowned

Ballymaloe Cookery School. The Butler's Pantry also identifies their competition as essentially any business that can provide an opportunity for consumers to buy food to go. This includes retailers with a convenience food offering, takeaways, garage forecourts and restaurants. Consumers are very convenience-driven, so they won't necessarily go out of their way to purchase the quality product provided by The Butler's Pantry. This is why the company is considering expanding its wholesale business to capture the consumer looking for a more convenient option.

BUILDING THE BRAND THROUGH STEADY GROWTH

Eileen Bergin was familiar with the food industry before establishing The Butler's Pantry: she had been involved in corporate catering and had taught cookery classes for a number of years. Coming from a family background where her father was an owner-manager, Eileen was well positioned to understand the difficulties of running your own business. However, she felt she had to pursue the business opportunity that she had identified for high-quality ready meals, as it was too good to miss. When the business started up it provided a small selection of ready meals and desserts. Right from the start Eileen focused on the quality and taste of the food produced. She felt that this focus on the food was central to the success of the business. The emphasis of the business was and still is on "real" food (see Appendix 6.2 for a sample menu from The Butler's Pantry). According to Eileen:

> There are no additives in our dishes and all ingredients are sources
> in Ireland and are fully traceable.

In the early stages, Eileen found she was putting in the very long hours typical of this stage of business development. It wasn't unusual to find her in work at 6.30 a.m. and not leaving until 10 p.m. Eileen found herself torn between family and work on an ongoing basis. Crucial to the success of the business was keeping focused on the business vision. Although the late 1980s was not the best time to launch a new business, particularly one in the high end of the food market, Eileen was convinced that the market would grow for her product.

Family and friends were very supportive of Eileen's business endeavours, and this encouragement helped increase her confidence in her ability to run the business. Despite initial difficulties Eileen did get some lucky breaks, for instance the location of the shop next door to a long-established off-licence gave an unexpected boost to the new business.

At the end of 1988 four people were employed in the business. The space needed by the business continued to grow so much that the landlord, who had an office on the premises, gave it up for the expanding business. The business continued to enjoy steady growth through developing a quality product and a strong reputation with its customers. Word of mouth was the primary means of developing the business in the early stages.

By 1991 The Butler's Pantry was seriously busy, and still no one else was following their lead. The business continued to develop until the time was right to open up another shop – in Donnybrook, in 1992. While the expansion was necessary, it posed additional logistical problems for the business: as the Donnybrook shop had no kitchen stock needed to be brought to it. The business had to invest in a van and recruit a part-time driver – a substantial investment at the time. The business continued its steady approach to growth under Eileen's direction until 1999, when she felt the need to expand the management team in order to expand the business.

Moving up a Gear

Eileen recognises that, while she has a strong influence on the business, other people are also crucial to its success. In 1999 Eileen made the decision to bring a new partner on board. She had thirty people working for the company at that stage and knew that, in order to manage the business effectively and plan for significant growth, new blood was needed. This was the obvious way to develop and grow the business, but it was not an easy decision, as it would involve giving up a share of the business.

Eileen identified that she needed a business partner who was passionate about the company and its ethos, as well as having the personality traits necessary to help the business to develop: vision, stubbornness and not taking 'no' for an answer being top of the list! Eileen didn't want to make any rash decisions about a new partner, she realised that a bad decision would be detrimental to the business, so she was ready to spend time on getting the right person. As she says herself:

I was determined to kiss a lot of frogs before I met the perfect prince or princess!

She put the feelers out among her business contacts and it was a Business Angel from Enterprise Ireland who suggested her new business partner, Jacquie Marsh. Eileen approached Jacquie and, after intense discussions over ten months, they agreed the terms for Jacquie to join the business.

The first activity for the new partnership was to develop a five-year business plan. This was fundamental in outlining where Eileen and Jacquie wanted to take the business and how they planned on getting there. The new addition to the management team gave the company the resources and the dynamic to expand the business more rapidly than ever before.

Eileen and Jacquie are not only interested in food as a profession, it is something that interests them personally as well. Jacquie is passionate about promoting healthy eating. She takes great pride in the fact that their food is "real" with a short shelf-life due to the lack of artificial preservatives.

Eileen is a member of the Slow Food Movement, an international association that promotes food and wine culture, opposes the standardisation of taste, defends the need for consumer information, protects cultural identities tied to food and gastronomic traditions, safeguards foods and cultivation and processing techniques inherited from tradition, and defends domestic and wild animals as well as vegetable species.

In addition to Eileen and Jacquie, there are now two other directors who are central to the business's development. In keeping with The Butler's Pantry's customer commitment of "natural ingredients, delicious recipes, hand prepared – from our kitchen to yours", the company's executive chef is part of the director team. The final director in the team is the financial controller, a critical part of any company's success.

It is not only the management team that contribute to the smooth running of the company, the rest of the staff are also essential to the quality of the business. The Butler's Pantry employs over fifty people and constantly aims to foster a good working atmosphere. The company believes it has the ability to get the best out of its employees and strives to make employees feel cared for. Testament to this ethos is the fact that three generations of the one family have worked in the business. The employees comprise an eclectic mix of mature and young people, graduates and early school leavers, and staff from many countries including Ireland, Ukraine, Poland and Egypt, making it an interesting and diverse place to work. As Jacquie says, "the staff are happy to work with and around a really good product".

Staff are encouraged to bring new ideas to their jobs and the company finds it gets real value from their input. This does not mean that the company has no staffing difficulties; like any business, good staff are headhunted. But through creating a positive and interesting work environment, staff turnover is kept to a minimum.

The management team is very hands-on and direct. One of the company's strengths is the fact that the management team thoroughly knows the business and its operations. Eileen identified early on that it is important for management to do everything initially so that they know every aspect of the business and can then support staff in their endeavours. She finds that her direct approach works well with staff as everyone knows where they stand. This is just one of the many traits she uses to manage The Butler's Pantry. When she started out, Eileen wanted to be the best in the business and employ happy people – something she hopes she has achieved.

The Skills to Succeed

Eileen admits that it was sometimes very tough to stay motivated in the early days.

> Sometimes I felt tired and fed up, especially when I seemed to be up against a brick wall, but that made me even more determined to succeed.

She finds it is easier now that the business is more established and has a strong team bringing it forward.

The business is a tribute to Eileen's determination to succeed in the face of seemingly insurmountable challenges. The chilled foods market was in its infancy when the business launched and there was no support available from enterprise support agencies or the banks when the business was getting established. Eileen felt this made her even more resolute in her determination that the business would be a success. In 1996, when Eileen was looking for finance for the third shop, the banks remained uninterested, despite the business being totally developed from cash flow and representing a profitable business model. "You have to be persistent and find a way to solve the problem", advises Eileen. Eileen does not feel she would still be in business today without her stubborn streak: she never takes no for an answer and feels there is always a way around a problem.

Eileen admits that she enjoys taking risks, albeit calculated ones, with the business.

> Every step of the way there's a risk. Employing my first employee was a risk – I didn't have a clue how to do it. Every time I have to borrow money is a risk, buying equipment, opening a new shop, I'm taking a risk. But despite being scared, I'm not going to stop... it makes me feel elated.

Eileen frequently re-evaluates her skills and is always looking to develop and refine her skills. She is an avid food reader and is constantly looking at the competition for ways of improving her product.

Right from the start, Eileen was clear about her business approach and this has formed the basis of the strategic direction of The Butler's Pantry. The starting point for any business in Eileen's view is that the business needs to be filling a real gap in the market – in her own words: "you need to have the right product at the right time for the right market". Once you have that established, you need to deliver the product or service consistently and really believe in the business, or it will not have a chance of success. The Butler's Pantry sees its key to success as being its quality and innovative product. The company goes to great lengths to ensure consistency in the product it offers. It constantly analyses the market both at home and abroad to spot new opportunities, such as developing a children's food range called "My Nosh". Always having fresh ideas and changing the food choices on offer is essential to keeping customers and attracting new ones, so new product development and innovation is key to The Butler's Pantry. The company has developed resources in-house and also works with the Dublin Institute of Technology, Enterprise Ireland and Bord Bia[4] to keep the products fresh and innovative.

A FOCUSED BUSINESS STRATEGY – THE KEY TO BUSINESS GROWTH

Since Jacquie joined Eileen in the business in 2000, The Butler's Pantry has been consistently growing, guided by five-year strategic plans. Eileen describes the development of the five-year plans as "the best thing we ever did". The management team dedicate a number of days each year to updating the strategic plan and ensuring they are meeting targets. While it is difficult to find the time to do this in a small business, the team recognise it is essential for the long-term success of the company, so they make sure to set aside the time necessary. The company recognise that the market is growing and they need to grow with it. The management team constantly monitor a series of key business indicators to keep track of the business performance. This information is used to ensure the implementation plans for business growth are on track (see Exhibit 6.1).

There are a number of different strands to the future growth of the business, namely expanding the wholesale market, increasing the number of shops and expanding product ranges and services. The company believes that positive sustainable growth takes time, so it has developed its strategic plan on this basis.

Expanding the Wholesale Market

The company started to get into the wholesale market in 1996 by placing their products in a few select delicatessens and supermarkets. It was essential

---

Exhibit 6.1
Key Business Performance Indicators

Key Indicator	Measures
Sales	• Average customer spend • Number of customers per shop • Breakdown of sales per product category
Food Cost	• Actual cost • Cost of food waste
Labour Cost	• Overall cost • Sales per man-hour • Sales per outlet
People – Customers	• Feedback • Number of complaints
People – Staff	• Number of days training • Number of new employees • Number of people leaving

Source: Interview with Jacquie Marsh, 26 January 2006

that the company kept control of the image and reputation of the brand, thus the development of the wholesale market has been slow and steady.

The business is eager to grow this aspect of turnover, but the desire for growth needs to be tempered with the need to protect the brand. Central to The Butler's Pantry's customer promise and its unique selling proposition (USP) is the handmade nature of its products, and this poses a dilemma for the business: can the company grow while maintaining its current business strength?

Increasing the Number of Shops

The company initially adopted a policy of slow and steady growth, opening three shops in its first ten years in business. This changed with the expansion of the management team, which has seen an additional three shops open in the past five years and plans to open a further two shops in 2006, and expand outside of the Dublin area.

A good location is key to the success of each of The Butler's Pantry's shops. The first shop was located in a residential area with a lot of passing trade. The criteria for the first shop has remained for the subsequent outlets, with premises located in areas identified by the director team as having high concentrations of their main customers: cash–rich, time–poor professionals. As well as selling its products, the shops provide a vehicle for customer feedback, taste testing, cookery demonstrations and special events, such as its celebration of Italian food, Festa Italiana, held in July 2006.

Product Range and Services

The company is constantly aware of the evolving characteristics of the marketplace and adapts its product offering accordingly. Recognising the growing trend of good food for children, The Butler's Pantry introduced their range of children's food, My Nosh, in 2004, with exciting names such as Mr McGregor's Pie, Pirates' Pie and Italian Yo Yos. The meals are in child-friendly portion sizes yet made from exactly the same fresh, high-quality ingredients as the classic adult meals.

As well as their main product list, The Butler's Pantry also caters for private and corporate events. Additionally, a cooking exhibition area in one of the shops has proved successful at attracting customers and the team is looking at possibly developing this option for other shops.

The company has always had a good attitude to change and views problems in the marketplace as opportunities for the business. Change is not seen as something to resist – staff are encouraged to try new things, with the emphasis being on continuous improvement rather than radical change. The company is very open to change and staff are constantly coming up with ideas on how to make improvements.

The business has big plans for the long-term. It would like to build a strong national brand and to continue to be producers and retailers of very fine quality food to go, while recruiting and retaining the best staff and continuing its trend in profitability. Ideally, The Butler's Pantry would like to expand nationally and then have a UK presence.

There are, of course, a number of challenges facing the business as it expands. Not least among these are the options to be considered for financing the business development. To date, the business has funded expansion using retained earnings, and has seen a steady increase in turnover over the past three years of about €0.5 million per annum to the expected turnover in 2006 of €3.5 million. Additionally, the company recognises that with growth comes more processes and procedures for all operations, for instance, now that the business has over fifty employees, the importance of developing a good human resource framework is critical.

What Does the Future Hold?

Despite the company's success, it cannot afford to be complacent. As well as increasing competition in both domestic and international markets, The Butler's Pantry faces a number of challenges to stay successful. Chief among these is managing business growth to balance product volume with both quality and the integrity of the product; in other words, can the business "stay special"? Will the company be able to keep its existing customers happy and manage the integrity of the brand while building new business? The management team have identified a number of possibilities for expansion and business development, but which approach should they focus on, or should they try a combination of approaches? What does The Butler's Pantry need to do to bring the business to the next stage of its development?

Acknowledgements

The author would like to thank Jacquie Marsh and Eileen Bergin of The Butler's Pantry for making this case study possible through generously giving their time and sharing information about their company.

References

Henchion, M. (2000) 'Meals for Cash Rich, Time Poor Consumers', paper presented at the Teagasc Ready Meals Conference, The Revolution in Convenience, June, Dublin available from: http://www.teagasc.ie/publications/readymeals2000/paper01.htm.

Mintel (2004) 'Report on Chilled Ready Meals', UK, May. Available from: www.mintel.com

Interviews

Bergin, Eileen and Marsh, Jacquie (2006): Managers of The Butler's Pantry, interview conducted 26 January 2006.

NOTES

1. This case was written as a basis for class discussion rather than to illustrate either effective or ineffective handling of an administrative situation.
2. Geraldine Lavin lectures at Dublin City University (DCU).
3. The Ashtown Food Research Centre (originally called the National Food Centre) was established in 1988 as a division of Teagasc, a semi-state organisation providing integrated research, advisory and training services for the agriculture and food industry in Ireland.
4. Bord Bia (Irish Food Board) is a semi-state organisation established in 1994 to act as a link between Irish food and drink suppliers and existing and potential customers. Its objective is to develop export markets for Irish food and drink companies and to bring the taste of Irish food to more tables worldwide.

Appendix 6.1: **Business Milestones**

1987	The Butler's Pantry establishes its first shop in Mount Merrion.
1991	The company increases its shop space in Mount Merrion Avenue, Blackrock.
1992	Second shop opens in Donnybrook. The company invests in a company van.
1995	The Butler's Pantry first receives the Bridgestone Award and continues to receive it every year since.
1996	Third shop opens in Temple Hill, Blackrock. Kitchen facilities are expanded with Mount Merrion Avenue housing the bakery and the Temple Hill premises catering for everything else.

	The shop in Mount Merrion Avenue is revamped. The company starts wholesaling the product into a limited number of carefully selected stores.
2000	A new partner joins the business. The development of the first five-year business plan.
2001	The bakery facility moves to the Temple Hill premises and the business acquires larger kitchen facilities in Bray. Establishment of guidelines and procedures to grow the business at a slow and steady pace.
2002	The company introduces more staff procedures, including induction training
2003	The Butler's Pantry is the small business award winner at the Irish Food and Drink Industry Awards.
2004	Fourth and fifth shops are opened in Sandymount and Clontarf. The Butler's Pantry is the small business award winner at the Irish Food and Drink Industry Awards again. "My Nosh" brand of children's food is launched.
2005	Sixth shop opens in Rathgar. The Butler's Pantry wins the Small Firms Association's National Retailer of the Year Award at the National Small Business Awards.
2006	The company moves all cooking production to bigger premises in Bray.

Source: Compiled from the company website (www.thebutlerspantry.ie) and interviews with Eileen Bergin and Jacquie Marsh, 26 January 2006.

Appendix 6.2: **Sample Menu**

Starters
- Crab potato cakes with garlic butter
- Duck rillette with balsamic & orange
- Goats' cheese & red pepper parcel
- Goats' cheese crostini with balsamic onions & watercress
- Pork & spinach terrine with onion jam

- Ricotta, leek & pine nut strudel
- Saffron & crab tart
- Smoked trout & salmon timbales

Main Courses

- Herb-crust chicken with green beans & roast pepper jus
- Braised lamb shanks with sun-dried tomatoes & French beans
- Beef filet Madagascar
- Beef filet with red-onion crust and rosti
- Angel-hair pasta with tiger shrimp, tomatoes, chilli & garlic
- Blackened salmon with black bean salsa
- Chilli roast salmon with cucumber pickle
- Orange and soy-glazed chicken with pak choy
- Pesto roast chicken with cherry tomato salsa
- Picatta of pork with parmesan and pesto

Desserts

- Hazelnut meringue roulade
- Coconut cream with Malibu fruits
- Mississippi meringue pie
- Chocolate crème brulée
- Raspberry and amaretto roulade
- Raspberry syllabub trifle
- Sherry trifle
- Strawberry meringue roulade
- Mocha roulade

Source: Compiled from company brochures and website (www.thebutlerspantry.ie)

GLENISK[1]

GERALDINE MCGING AND PAULINE CONNOLLY[2]

"**A** busy week at the office!" thought Vincent Cleary. It was the end of the third week in June 2006 and Vincent was pondering on the recent development in his family business. 37 per cent of Glenisk had just been bought by Stonyfield Europe, and his company was about to receive an enormous injection of cash into what had become a very successful enterprise. Although Vincent would not disclose the actual financial deal, suffice to say that he was a happy man. As Vincent left the office he reflected on the ironic situation that was unfolding. Thinking back on a time when most Irish farmers were heavily dependant upon grant aid and subsidies from Europe, his father, the late John (Jack) Cleary, saw an entrepreneurial opportunity that now resulted in his family business becoming a part of one of the leading global food producers. "If my Dad was here now, he would be proud and think of this as a job well done", thought Vincent. "Who could have imagined that in June 2006, Stonyfield Europe – 80 per cent owned by Danone and 20 per cent by Stonyfield Farm – would buy a 37 per cent stake in Glenisk, Ireland's biggest organic fresh dairy products producer? Yes," he thought, "it was indeed a busy day at the office".

Yogurt is a fermented milk that was first sold as an aid to digestion but has since developed into a 'must stock' for retailers and appears to have benefited from an increase in the public's awareness of health and well-being. The recent developments at Glenisk did not happen by accident. Sound business planning sprinkled with a dusting of entrepreneurial good fortune brought about the success that would see Glenisk organic yogurt become available worldwide. While the Cleary family continue to manage Glenisk, a number of challenges and opportunities lie ahead for this company, including taking advantage of the investors' marketing experience, realising the benefit of their distributors' network and dealing with the management issues that will need to be considered as the company develops.

BACKGROUND

Glenisk produce and make available to the Irish market a wide range of organic dairy produce utilising fully certified Irish organic milk. The business was set up by a County Offaly farmer to provide employment for his fourteen children. It has evolved into three separate enterprises, one of which – the loss leader – posed a threat to the entire operation in the mid-nineties. This loss leader, however, has subsequently developed into a multi-million euro generator of sales (see Exhibit 7.1). But it did not arrive at this profitable stage without having tumbled through the highs and lows of tough decision-making, rigorous planning and sheer dedication.

The late Jack Cleary ran his farm with enthusiasm and in 1979–80 he set up a creamery, Tullamore Dairies, to process the milk yield from his farm. In 1987 he expanded the business to include yogurt production and Glenisk was formed. This yogurt-making company enjoyed early success,

---

Exhibit 7.1
Glenisk's Achievements

No. 1 Organic yogurt brand in Ireland
Brand growth of +40% year on year
3.5m+ litres of organic milk per year
4,000+ tons of yogurt per year
10% share of the total Irish yogurt market
Turnover by product type

    ✓90% ORGANIC

     ✓10% CONVENTIONAL (Goats' Milk Products)

Source: Cleary, Vincent. Proceedings of the Green Ireland Conference, Kilkenny Castle, 16–18 June 2006, *Glenisk Organic Ireland,* viewed 10 September 2006, <http://www.gmfreeireland.org/conference/PPT/Glenisk.ppt>

---

securing contracts with Quinnsworth, the predecessor of what is now Tesco Ireland. Other supermarket multiples also bought the yogurt and within six months Glenisk had captured 5 per cent of the Irish yogurt market. For the next six years little changed within the Glenisk product portfolio; no research and development or product development took place and the business stagnated. Sales dwindled and by 1994 it was clear that the company was in financial trouble.

Sadly, in 1995 Jack Cleary died, leaving behind a loss-making family business. At that time, no management structure was in place and family members had conflicting views in relation to the future direction of the estate. Finally, two of the brothers took over and formed a committee to run the company. The current joint Managing Director, Vincent Cleary's view of the committee was that "it was an all-male Cleary ensemble, following the old family pecking order of the eldest ruling the roost – it was never going to work".

It soon became evident to the company's accountants that the committee did not possess the management style or skill to lead the enterprise forward. The accountants' advice was clear. Glenisk was a loss maker with no sign of becoming profitable in the foreseeable future. Therefore, the company should cease trading in order to save the farm and Tullamore Dairies.

The two younger brothers, Vincent and Brendan, saw an opportunity and offered to take the loss-making yogurt company from the committee while the two eldest brothers saw this as a chance to shed their loss-making company, allowing them to return to concentrating on farming. No cash changed hands between the brothers, as the late Jack Cleary had left cross-ownership of the companies and lands so it was a 'straight swap', which received the Revenue Commissioners' approval. In 1997 Glenisk continued trading under a new management structure.

Today it employs twenty-eight people, supplies organic dairy produce to the Irish market and is turning over €7.5 million. The company has recently been awarded €1.3 million worth of press advertising as a result of winning a competition sponsored by Bord Bia and the NNI (National Newspapers of Ireland). No advertising award, however, compares to the enormous impact the investment by Stonyfield Europe will have on this company and many changes are forecast to take place. In order to appreciate the successful path this company has taken it is appropriate to look back on the business environment in which Glenisk developed.

IRELAND TODAY

Ireland has enjoyed great economic growth over the last decade. In his budget speech in 2005, the Minister for Finance Brian Cowen stated that, "we are living in the midst of the longest and strongest era of sustained prosperity in all of Irish history. This didn't happen by chance... As a nation we now enjoy a much-enhanced quality of life. We are a prosperous country. More of our citizens are in work than at any time in our history. More enjoy a decent quality of life than ever before".

A reflection upon the events of the 1970s and 1980s, set against modern Ireland in 2006 is important, if only as a reminder to the new generation who know nothing other than the Celtic Tiger. One in five people in the state at that time were without a job. The crisis in Irish state finances was so alarming that there was talk of asking the World Bank to intervene to rescue the country from its' state of potential bankruptcy. Emigration was seen by many as the only way to secure a future and the 'brain drain' was a reflection of this.

Vincent Cleary was part of this generation. In 1981 he completed his Leaving Certificate and in 1986 he headed off to seek his fortune in Limerick. At that time, while he did not want to farm the home place, he had not identified any particular career path that he wished to follow. He began working for another family business, Shannon Dairies, just outside of Limerick. Vincent returned home in 1987 for a few months for the launch of Glenisk, but things did not work out between his father and himself, so he left again – this time he departed for Germany. Father and son reconciled their differences in 1992; Vincent was just married and had introduced his new wife to the family and to Ireland. In 1993 the late Jack Cleary invited Vincent back to County Offaly, and he subsequently returned in 1994.

THE GERMAN EXPERIENCE

Vincent Cleary arrived in Germany with no third level qualification, no skill or trade and no work experience behind him. He says of his working life there:

> I was employed initially at nothing too distinguished but made
> my way up the corporate ladder through hard work and sheer

determination. However, my heart never left Ireland and I jumped at the opportunity to return there.

During his time in Germany, Vincent was able to observe a country which, in the 1980s, was doing very well economically and was the driving force of Europe. In a frank interview, he commented:

It was a great learning experience to be in a country where I could observe marketing in action. For example, as a patriotic Irish lad in a foreign country I was watching and admiring Kerrygold and their marketing efforts in Germany. However, I often felt that there were opportunities that Kerrygold were missing, especially on the organic front. I often watched the German family unit and how they did their shopping at the weekends and how it differed so much to the typical Irish family upbringing I had back in Ireland. The family of mother, father and one child gave the youngster the best of everything – which was possible for Ireland if we had such disposable income. If a German dad wore an Armani suit, the child was attired in as good a brand suitable for children. The child's diet was the best that money could buy: organic, no additives and very healthy. Perhaps it was a guilt factor because both parents were working, or maybe it was just because they had the money. But the Germans also looked after their bodies in the diet that they consumed. Sometimes I felt Kerrygold were missing opportunities. At that time, the organic movement was snowballing on the continent and the Germans viewed Ireland as the wild west of Europe, more akin to "Frontier country" rather than "Cowboy country" (that tag came later). They saw it as the best place to find green and organic products.

Vincent continued:

I remember in 1989 a German businessman went on television and he told the German public that he would be sourcing organic vegetables and other raw organic ingredients for baby food in Ireland. While that was a very good plug for both Ireland and

Irish vegetables (because the Germans equated Ireland with a very green image), I expect he got a bit of a shock when he couldn't source organic products when he arrived on the Emerald Isle!

COMPANY STRUCTURE

The Cleary brothers were able to negotiate successfully many of the pitfalls that can arise in family-run businesses and had the benefit of strong leadership in their choice of joint managing directors. Vincent and Brendan have led the company from a state of bankruptcy to the profitable position it is in today. Vincent commented that:

> Once Brendan is convinced that my ideas contain merit, I feel that convincing the rest of the family is just a formality. There have been days when the family have given me the silent treatment because of decisions I have made, but this is just another part of business. As a businessperson, I have to get on with it and not take it personally.

Vincent also commented that he can see a new vision coming from the next generation of the Cleary family who have joined the company since it was "taken back" under a clear management structure. They do not question success, but take it for granted. This will certainly help lead the company in its future developmental stages.

Vincent admits that, at times, building the management team was difficult:

> I accept that I became quite bullish insofar as pushing my own ideas down other siblings' throats. I am still, on occasion, accused of being non-communicative to some siblings, although this bullishness has been crucial to our collective success

He continued, "entrepreneurship requires moments of ruthlessness". For example, he said:

> I accept that it has not always been easy with a group of nine family members working together, as well as our other employees, and

I have faced days when all other siblings have 'ganged-up' on me. Nevertheless, I have grown to understand that sometimes it's best just to let the defeats go by without paying too much attention to them.

He recalls that one of the first battles he won, with the joint managing director's support, was to insist that organic cows' milk be the key ingredient for Glenisk Yogurt.

Today, the management structure of Glenisk is very clear, with all siblings taking responsibility for key aspects of the organisation's operation, although none of the family had any prior management experience. The Joint Managing Directors are still Brendan and Vincent Cleary. Brendan is also the main yogurt maker. Gerard Cleary is an accountant and also the Financial Director. The Administration Manager is Evelyn Cleary, who is the only sister involved in the company. There are two Directors of Production, Mark Cleary and Brian Cleary. Vincent commented, "Mark is 'coming into his own', and is an important back-room player; in many respects he is 'Mr Sellotape' as he sticks all aspects of the day-to-day running of the business together". Vincent also stated that Brian is key to the smooth day-to-day running of Glenisk. As a footnote, Vincent commented that:

My only gripe is that my production siblings tend to think that the world starts and ends with production – I believe that this is the belief of most production people on a global basis.

Other members of the management team include Thomas Donohue, Engineering Manager, and Cora Neary, Laboratory Manager.

STONYFIELD EUROPE

Group Danone is a leading global food producer. It is a global leader in three strong-growth categories: fresh dairy products, bottled water, and biscuits and cereal products. It employs 89,449 people in 120 countries and in 2004 recorded sales of €13,700 million. In 2006 it formed Stonyfield Europe with Stonyfield, a leading American organic dairy farm. The company's first acquisition was a 37 per cent share in Glenisk. The chief executive officer of Stonyfield Farm and now chairman of

Stonyfield Europe, Gary Hirshberg, said the new venture aims to help Glenisk increase its production capacity and marketing:

> It is also Stonyfield Europe's first step in our own agenda of lever-aging our 23-year US experience on behalf of family farmers and consumers to help catalyse the development and expansion of sim-ilar grassroots organic enterprises (www.stonyfield.com/AboutUs/ MoosReleases_Display.cfm?pr_id=122).

Danone had planned to launch a new range of organic yogurts in Europe, made by Stonyfield Farm, in which it acquired an 80 per cent stake in 2004. They were in the process of investing €52 million into the Stonyfield plant in New Hampshire in order to increase production capac-ity to cope with its new export market. Danone said it intended to use the launch to capitalise on growing demand for organic dairy products but had not yet settled on a European brand name or distribution plan. Franck Riboud, chairman and chief executive of Danone, said:

> The European market for organic dairy products is growing, but it remains a fairly discreet presence. With Stonyfield Europe, we hope to capitalise on the success and unique expertise of Stonyfield Farm to speed up its development (www.stonyfield.com/AboutUs/ MoosReleases_Display.cfm?pr_id=122).

THE PRODUCTS

Glenisk manufacture and supply a wide range of dairy products to the Irish marketplace, including probiotic organic yogurt, in different flavours and different fat levels, fresh goats' milk and yogurt, fresh organic cows' milk and organic cream. Organic has been the defining characteristic of Glenisk's development (see Exhibit 7.2). This means that the main ingredients are up to 50 per cent more expensive than non-organic products on the market. The term "organic" is used to describe agricultural products that use no pesti-cides or synthetic fertilisers. Organic methods consider the whole ecosys-tem and use natural techniques to assist plant growth, repel pests and protect and encourage wildlife habitats. Organic agriculture aims to maintain and increase soil fertility and give livestock humane living conditions.

On average, organic food contains higher levels of naturally occurring Omega oils, vitamin C and essential minerals such as calcium, magnesium,

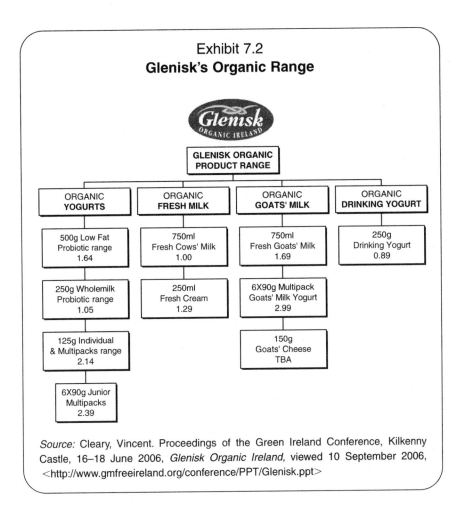

Exhibit 7.2
Glenisk's Organic Range

Source: Cleary, Vincent. Proceedings of the Green Ireland Conference, Kilkenny Castle, 16–18 June 2006, *Glenisk Organic Ireland,* viewed 10 September 2006, <http://www.gmfreeireland.org/conference/PPT/Glenisk.ppt>

iron and chromium. Many researchers from around the world have identified that organic crops have statistically significantly higher levels of vitamin C, magnesium, iron and phosphorous. Spinach, lettuce, cabbage and potatoes showed particularly high levels of minerals. Scientists from Glasgow University have found a link between the levels of nitrates in vegetables and gullet cancer, which has trebled over the last twenty years and claims more than 3,000 lives a year. They believe that an increase in the use of nitrate fertilisers since World War II may be one of the main reasons for the rise in this cancer. Organic cows' milk is now supplied to Glenisk by forty organic farmers located all around the country.

The supply of goats' milk came about by accident. Vincent Cleary rescued a donkey that needed a home. To keep it company, he put two goats in the field that also needed a home. The milk from these two goats led to the first fresh Glenisk goats' milk available in Ireland. Glenisk goats' milk is now supplied by fifteen commercial farmers who are located all around the country.

Not all entrepreneurial success is as a result of meticulous planning. The goats' milk story is indicative of this. Vincent recalls:

> I was sitting at meeting with some buyers discussing Glenisk yogurt, who were quite clearly in no rush to conclude the meeting. One of the buyers noticed me looking at my watch and inquired whether I was under pressure. In the most bashful way possible, I explained that I had to return home as the goats had to be milked. At this time my German wife was looking for a job, so I asked her would she fancy milking goats!

This romantic invitation started Glenisk as a major supplier of fresh goats' milk to retailers. Up until this point, much of the goats' milk supplied in Ireland was frozen to ensure continuity of supply. According to Vincent, in the early days he "fought with his siblings over the small volumes of goats' milk going through the system. Some of them were on for knocking the line before it got up and running". Goats' milk now represents 20–25 per cent of the total turnover at Glenisk.

COMPETITORS AND THE MARKETPLACE

Until 1997 the yogurt market in Ireland was dominated by the Yoplait brand, owned by Glanbia. That year saw the introduction of a new brand, Danone. Currently the market is divided between Danone, which has the largest share of the yogurt market, Yoplait and Müller. Glenisk have now achieved fourth place. In the mid-1990s, Yeo Valley were market leaders in the supply of organic yogurt in Ireland, however Glenisk have now secured that position. The main competitors for Glenisk are Danone and Yoplait, the conventional yogurt brands. According to Vincent:

> We are not only competing with organic labels but also with the conventional yoghurt brands.

The fresh dairy market in Ireland has an estimated worth of more than €200 million, and is growing by 24 per cent year-on-year. It has evolved rapidly from a traditional homogenous one to a contemporary segmented one and the natural health sector (especially probiotics) is now the fastest growing sector in the category with 59 per cent annual growth. The natural health sector now accounts for 28 per cent of total category sales with products such as 100 per cent natural yogurt, probiotic yogurts, organic yogurts and probiotic yogurt drinks.

As a result of the Stonyfield Europe investment in Glenisk, it remains to be seen if the brand name Glenisk will be maintained and will continue to compete directly with Danone, or will a new brand be developed to facilitate the expected future growth of organic dairy products for the European market.

Marketing Strategy

Irish people are being bombarded with marketing messages on how to live longer, boost immune systems, look younger, achieve lower cholesterol levels and lose weight. In essence, consumers only have to visit their local supermarket to find products that promise to do wonders for their health and well-being. Suppliers and producers of health-associated products have realised that there is a market there to be exploited to meet the consumers' needs, and are investing their marketing resources in the promotion of health-boosting products. The yogurt market, in particular, has benefited from this interest in healthy living, especially yogurts that not only taste good but also offer health benefits to the consumer. For example, probiotic yogurts contain special cultures that are said to aid digestion or help boost the body's immune system.

Cleary suggests there are five key mega-trends driving food category growth in the last five years:

- Health: a well-being trend through the creation of "FOOD PLUS" Products (something added) and "FOOD MINUS" products (i.e. No-Fat, No Sugar), also more "Natural" and "Pure" type products.
- Vegetarian and organic.
- Convenience and snacking: more convenience and snacking-type products – "No time to sit down and eat", smaller snacking portion sizes.
- Indulgence foods: premium products, new more exotic flavours, new ethnic varieties and a rise in pure indulgence-type products.

- Product presentation: improved packaging (resealability, recyclable, stand-up packs, improved print graphics, better shelf presence, new pack sizes and shapes, etc.).

There is no doubt that the recent investment in Glenisk is going to have a major impact on the marketing plans that Glenisk may have had in the past. Vincent Cleary said that he realised that a marketing strategy is an integral part of gaining market share. He admits that, although in 2005 they spent half a million euros on promotion, they do not have a marketing strategy. The marketing budget did not allow for an advertising budget, so they have struggled to maintain a high profile in a heavily advertised industry.

Danone are regarded as the biggest investors in advertising. They have invested heavily in television advertising using scientific references to explain how the cultures in their products work. Their marketing aim is to maximise sales by having products available that appeal to people of all ages and lifestyles. Yoplait responded to the challenges posed by Danone by introducing its own probiotic yogurt drink as well as expanding its existing range of fruit yogurts and fromage frais. Like Danone, Yoplait carried out an extensive advertising campaign including both television and radio advertisements.

THE FUTURE OF GLENISK

After the investment in Glenisk was announced, Vincent Cleary said:

> We've been approached over the years by other companies interested in Glenisk, but if five or even ten years ago I had to name my top choice in terms of partners, it would have been Stonyfield because of its commitment to organics and record of success . . . With Stonyfield Farm Glenisk will find its way to the next level of our own development. This investment comes after a lot of soul-searching, probably due to the fact that we're family operators, with personal histories tied to the company, but Glenisk will evolve into a stronger entity as a result.

So what direction will Glenisk take for the future? A major player in the European food market has purchased 37 per cent of the company for an undisclosed sum of money. In 2004, the same company bought 80 per cent of Stonyfield Farm in the US. It could be interpreted that Danone are about to target in a major way the entire organic dairy market. The main question that needs to be addressed, however, is how long will it be before Stonyfield Europe puts pressure on Glenisk and buys out the company completely. This could be identified in a positive way: that is the directors of Glenisk could be viewed as true entrepreneurs, identifying an opportunity, taking a risk, developing the product and bringing it to market, and then selling on the concept to another company while they start out on a new entrepreneurial venture.

On the other hand, if the Cleary family want to maintain their share of the company, this may prove to be a challenging management issue for Glenisk. The company will benefit enormously from the marketing experience and distribution networks Danone has established, as well as its production know-how.

Glenisk has survived management challenges in the past. The directors must have a clear view on what they want from the company now and in the future. Some issues that need consideration include perceived expectations of the investment, valuation expectations of the company and the strength of the management team and their personal ties to Glenisk.

Interviews

Cleary Vincent (2005–2006): Joint MD of Glenisk, interviews conducted 8 December 2005, 31 January 2006 and 22 June 2006.

NOTES

1. This case was written as a basis for class discussion rather than to illustrate either effective or ineffective handling of an administrative situation.
2. Geraldine McGing and Pauline Connolly lecture at Griffith College Dublin.